CHALLENGES OF THE THIRD AGE

CHALLENGES OF THE THIRD AGE

Meaning and Purpose in Later Life

Edited by
ROBERT S. WEISS
&
SCOTT A. BASS

OXFORD
UNIVERSITY PRESS

2002

OXFORD

UNIVERSITY PRESS

Oxford   New York
Athens   Auckland   Bangkok   Bogotá   Buenos Aires   Cape Town
Chennai   Dar es Salaam   Delhi   Florence   Hong Kong   Istanbul   Karachi
Kolkata   Kuala Lumpur   Madrid   Melbourne   Mexico City   Mumbai   Nairobi
Paris   São Paulo   Shanghai   Singapore   Taipei   Tokyo   Toronto   Warsaw

and associated companies in
Berlin   Ibadan

Published by Oxford University Press, Inc.
198 Madison Avenue, New York, New York 10016

Oxford is a registered trademark of Oxford University Press.

Library of Congress Cataloging-in-Publication Data
Challenges of the third age : meaning and purpose in later life /
edited by Robert S. Weiss and Scott A. Bass.
p.   cm.
Includes bibliographical references and index.
ISBN 0-19-513339-0; ISBN 0-19-515025-2 (pbk.)
1. Self-actualization (Psychology) in old age.   2. Aged—Psychology.   3. Meaning
(Psychology)   I. Weiss, Robert Stuart, 1925–   II. Bass, Scott A.
BF724.85.S45 C48 2000
305.26—dc21   00-027170

1 3 5 7 9 8 6 4 2

Printed in the United States of America
on acid-free paper

Contents

Contributors

SCOTT A. BASS is Dean of the Graduate School and Vice Provost for Research at the University of Maryland, Baltimore County (UMBC), where he also holds academic appointments of Distinguished Professor of Sociology and Policy Sciences. Dr. Bass is an expert in the field of gerontology and has published over fifty book chapters and thirty monographs or research reports on aging and aging policy.

BERTRAM J. COHLER is William Rainey Harper Professor, The College, the Committee on Human Development, and the Department of Psychology, University of Chicago. Together with Robert Galatzer-Levy, he is author of *The Course of Lesbian and Gay Lives: Psychoanalytic and Social Perspectives.*

ROSE DOBROF is Brookdale Professor of Gerontology at Hunter College. She was the founding Director of the Hunter/Brookdale Center on Aging and was a member of the faculty at the Hunter College School of Social Work from 1964 until 1975.

DAVID GUTMANN, as an academic psychologist, studies the normal development of the aging personality in this and other cultures. As a clinical psychologist, he studies the abnormal psychology of aging—particularly those conditions that result from failures of normal development in the later years. He is currently studying the ways aging kibbutz members manage the transition to retired life.

ANDREW J. HOSTETLER is an advanced doctoral student in the Committee on Human Development, University of Chicago. He is completing his dissertation studying the lives of presently single and partnered middle-aged and older gay men. He is collaborating with Bertram Cohler on a continuing study of the lived experience of middle-aged gay men and women.

PETER MARRIS was associated with the Institute of Community Studies, London, for seventeen years, and then the Centre for Environmental Studies, before joining the Urban Planning Program at the University of California, Los Angeles. He has taught at the University of California, Berkeley, M.I.T., Boston University, University of Massachusetts Boston, Brandeis University, Makerere University, and Yale, where he is presently a lecturer. He has undertaken research on housing and local economic development, community action, and loss in Britain, the United States, and in East and West Africa.

HARRY R. MOODY is National Program Director for the Faith in Action Program of the Robert Wood Johnson Foundation. He was for many years at the Brookdale Center on Aging of Hunter College, where he served as Executive Director. Harry Moody is the author of several books on bioethics, social policy, and aging, and, most recently, *The Five Stages of the Soul,* a monograph on spiritual development in the second half of life. He is Chairman of the Board of the national Elderhostel organization.

ROBERT MORRIS is Professor Emeritus at Brandeis University, an educator, and a social policy consultant. He is Editor-in-

Chief of the *16th Edition of the Encyclopedia of Social Work and Welfare*, and author (or editor) of *Social Policy of the American Welfare State; Rethinking Social Welfare; Feasible Planning for Social Change; Centrally Planned Change; the National Government and Social Welfare: What Should be the Federal Role?; Welfare Report 1996–2000: Is There a Safety Net?;* and *Personal Assistance and the Future of Home Care.*

HEGE RAVDAL is a student in the Ph.D. Program in Gerontology at the University of Kentucky. With a background in anthropology and geography, her research interests currently include aging in rural environments, family caregiving to elders with dementia, aging and ethnicity, and crosscultural social gerontology. She pursues these through a life-course perspective using qualitative methodologies.

GRAHAM D. ROWLES is Professor of Geography and Behavioral Science, Director of the Ph.D. Program in Gerontology, and Associate Director of the Sanders-Brown Center on Aging at the University of Kentucky. His research focuses on the experience of aging in different environmental contexts. A central theme of this work is exploration, employing qualitative methodologies, of the changing relationship between elders and their environment with advancing age and the implications of this relationship for health and well-being.

ROBERT L. RUBINSTEIN is Professor of Anthropology at the University of Maryland, Baltimore County (UMBC). A cultural anthropologist, Rubinstein has conducted many research projects on old age and aging in the United States. His current research concerns death and dying in nursing homes.

RICHARD A. SETTERSTEN, JR. is Assistant Professor and Director of Graduate Study in the Department of Sociology at Case

Western Reserve University. Most of his work relates to the theoretical and methodological challenges associated with studying aging and the life course. He is the author of *Lives in Time and Place: The Problems and Promises of Developmental Science.*

ROBERT S. WEISS is Professor Emeritus of Sociology, University of Massachusetts Boston, and Senior Fellow of the Gerontology Institute at the University. He was also for many years a member of Harvard Medical School's Laboratory of Community Psychiatry. He has authored and coauthored nine books and seventy papers, most of them dealing with the ways people respond to new life situations.

CHALLENGES OF THE THIRD AGE

Introduction

Robert S. Weiss and Scott A. Bass

The post-retirement years are, for many, a time when there is no longer responsibility for childcare nor need for paid employment, the two obligations that would have structured much of preceding life. Many in these retirement years have available to them pensions and savings adequate to maintain middle income styles of life and, in addition, health and energy not much diminished from their later years of employment. Their freedom and resources permit them to enter into any of a very wide range of activities. To an extent remarkable outside the realm of the very rich, they can fashion lives to suit themselves.

The life phase in which there is no longer employment and childraising to commandeer time, and before morbidity enters to limit activity and mortality brings everything to a close, has been called the Third Age. Those in this phase of life have passed through a first age of youth, when they prepared for the activities of maturity, and a second age of maturity, when their lives were given to those activities, and have reached a third age in which they can, within fairly wide limits, live their lives as they please, before being overtaken by a fourth age of decline.

The Third Age came into being through the conjunction of two happy developments. The first is increased national wealth that is being realized by many among the middle class now of retirement age through pensions and savings and capital gains from homes bought cheap and sold dear. To be sure, the distribution of increased national wealth does not extend to those of retirement age who had earlier worked at low-income jobs or worked only sporadically, but it extends quite widely nevertheless. The second happy development is an augmented longevity that extends the normal life expectancy for several years and, even more important, extends for several years the expectancy of a life not handicapped by physical limitation.

But the Third Age ensures only that there is "freedom from": freedom from the demands of earlier life, freedom from the need to earn a living, freedom from responsibilities for others. The question then becomes, for the witnessing society and for those who are themselves experiencing the Third Age, what is it a time of freedom for?

Those in the Third Age have the opportunity to decide what is meaningful in life apart from work and childraising and to devote to it their final years of full activity. Many possibilities are available to them. Some will find new sources of meaning in the excitement and challenge of travel and adventure, or in self-realization through voluntary activities or further education or the pursuit of crafts or arts, or in the celebration of domesticity through gardening and housekeeping and projects around the house. Some may try to retain a part of what had earlier been meaningful and find a way to continue in the world of work, though on a reduced scale so that other activities remain possible. Some, through grandparenting, will function as part-time parents, though again with diminished responsibilities. But some will essentially say there is nothing in life as meaningful as full engagement with work or genuine responsibility for parenting (or grandparenting), and they will try to fend off change and retain their full schedule of responsibility and associated social importance or, failing this, lapse into disengagement and despair.

This book is an examination of the issues raised by the emergence of the Third Age, and especially the issues implied by the question "What is the Third Age for?" Our authors consider how the issues of the Third Age are different from issues encountered earlier in life; how our society understands (and fails to understand) the issues of the Third Age and what have been its changing ideas about this time of life; what meanings are given to this time of life in other societies and in enclaves just off the mainstream of our own society; and how individuals in the Third Age and just beyond the Third Age make sense of their lives.

Our impression is that many in the Third Age find life to be enjoyable and satisfactory yet often feel themselves not fully engaged. They work on their homes and care for their grandchildren or, if their grandchildren live far away, visit them or are visited by them. Always there is the possibility of a crisis, perhaps an illness or injury, more often an illness in the family, or a child's divorce. Then they are fully absorbed in helping, often resentful that they must even while they are grateful that they are able to. Without a crisis, some seem just to let time go by, trying for a pleasant afternoon, an interesting evening, and not much more. There can easily be drift: letting things happen, deciding on activities one at a time and so establishing a routine that is good enough, but not at all chosen.

One of us (Weiss) has interviewed almost a hundred people entering or in the Third Age. One of the few respondents in the study who seemed thoroughly realized in his postretirement activities was a man who had sold his small business in order to become a craftsman in wood. He earlier had rejected the prospect of a retirement in which, as he put it, the high point of the day would be deciding where to have dinner. Now he was doing something he cared about. But he is clear about what he did not want for his retirement:

> We'd gone to Florida for three years, and when we visited last year, we stayed with friends for three weeks, and that was more than we could take. The fellow, he read the newspaper in the morning for about two and a half hours. Then we went for a walk. After that we took the ladies shopping. And finally we sat around and discussed where we would eat dinner. And we went through that for four, five days.
>
> Then we moved on to stay with other friends. This fellow, I guess he's got arthritis, so he sits in the bathtub for an hour and a half in the morning. Then he gets on the phone and talks to his broker for two hours. Then he plays cards for a while. Then we discuss where we're going to have dinner.
>
> It seemed all of our friends do that down there. And that appalls me. I have to be doing something constructive.

This respondent recognized and rejected a life of drift, of trying for a pleasant day and evening and not much more. He wanted engagement to which he could give himself whole-heartedly. He also wanted to engage in an activity that others would recognize as valuable, that might even make a difference for them as well as for himself. He had known for some time that he enjoyed crafts, and especially working with wood. Working with wood, he decided, would be what he would retire to.

> I'm an engineer by education. And when I was in college they had what they called shop, where you had to go through all the steps of making a wooden pattern for castings. Then there was a foundry on the campus where you made the molds and cast the metal, then you went into a machine shop and machined this. And working in the woodworking shop, I just really enjoyed that. And it always stayed with me from then on.

I always did something with wood. Never anything great, on the order of making furniture, but I could pass for a carpenter, I guess. For example, I had an old-fashioned fireplace and two windows above it. I tore all that out and rebuilt it and built a new mantelpiece. I put in a playroom for the children in the basement. If you have a little bit of nerve, you tackle something, knowing that if you get into trouble you can go out and find yourself a carpenter to save you.

Probably five years before I retired, when I was fifty-seven, I said, "I think I'd like to work with wood and make furniture when I retire." So I started just formulating the idea of what I would like to do. And just everything worked out well and on time.

The respondent used the first year of his retirement to obtain instruction in furniture making. When we talked with him two years later, he said he achieved great satisfaction from what he now felt to be his work. He was serious about the enterprise. It wasn't a hobby. Almost, it was a calling.

I turn out furniture, and I'm proud of it, because it comes out right. And if it doesn't go well, I throw it away and I start another piece of wood. There's nobody looking over my shoulder, so there's no pressure. I have to please myself primarily. And I don't have to make money. But I work hard at it, and I think it looks good. I know where all the bad spots are, and I hope nobody will notice them.

The fact that someone compliments me, it's very satisfying. That's my reward, really. If I was making footstools and plant stands, nothings, and people went into great ecstasies over them, I'd know they're insincere. But I make complex pieces of furniture.

I never hated what I was doing, even when it was tough. I didn't dread getting up in the morning. But after you do it for forty years, you get a little bit tired of the same thing. Maybe I'll get tired of doing woodworking. I don't know.

I don't see it yet. Because there are a lot of things I haven't done yet that I want to try. It's a craft, and you keep improving it, and there are still things you haven't done yet.

The respondent no longer works for money, but he does continue to work, in the sense that he continues to give his energy to socially useful production. He has, indeed, found an enterprise that meets his needs, as his career employment no longer did. Making fine furniture provides challenge, an outlet for a creative, even artistic impulse, and an opportunity for recognition. That the final products hardly pay for the wood and tools and shop space that went into their making, let alone for the time spent on them, matters little.

Other respondents held part-time jobs in occupations that stretched in social prestige from delivery person to college lecturer. Often they valued their work for providing them with a role in ongoing society and at the same time valued that the work was only part-time, so they still had freedom to do other things or to do nothing at all.

For those who continued to work, including the few who continued with full-time work, work had different meanings from those it had had earlier in life. No longer was their work required for support of a family; they worked, possibly, because they needed to augment their incomes but, more likely, it seemed, because they wanted to. They were senior figures in their work groups, recognized as at the end of their careers. And what lay ahead of them, in the world of work, was not youth's apparently endless prospect but rather an uncertain, but surely limited, time of continued capability.

Changed relationships to others can pose problems of meaning for those in the Third Age. For many, life's meaning had been found in the assumption of responsibility for others. Responsibilities to family members are likely to continue in the Third Age but much diminished from what they once were. If all has gone well with one's children, their respect should remain; indeed, there is much to be said for having the wealth or the strength of character to play the patriarch or matriarch to the end. And yet a special role in the family, while important, is unlikely by itself to make life meaningful; it isn't the same as being a responsible parent of dependent children.

Nor is it nearly as effortless as it might once have been to command the respect of strangers. Age alone can signal irrelevance. And there may well no longer be a job title to establish social place.

Association with others may diminish. Those who have left their primary career will be without the engagements that for years had constituted a social world. Some, like the respondent quoted, will find alternative uses of creative energy that will bring about new associations. But others are likely to become dependent for social engagement on their husbands and wives, their friends, and their spread-out families. If these associations attenuate, because of losses due to disability and death, or simply because lives take different directions, there is risk of disengagement and isolation.

Yet if the threat of the postretirement years is that of no longer mattering to oneself or others, there is also promise in the extraordinary freedom of these years. There is opportunity for the pleasure of new and varied experience through travel. It is possible to buy a recreational vehicle and go wherever climate and whim suggest. There is opportunity for self-development through education in arts or humanities or new fields of work. There is opportunity to spend time with children and grandchildren and opportunity for the quiet gratifications of tending one's home and garden. The question is whether any of these opportunities can be utilized to provide lives of authenticity and richness and value.

Many in the Third Age find ways of being of service to others. One of our respondents gave a good deal of time to functioning as a lay minister, another to helping new members of AA. A respondent whose income was quite low, compared to the incomes of others who had been in middle-income occupations, used his pickup truck to do shopping for neighbors and to provide supplies for a neighborhood church's charitable food distributions. A respondent who had been a skilled carpenter, as well as an instructor in a trade school, now used his skills to complete projects for members of his family.

Contributions to others tended to use skills that in some way sustained respondents' self-image as useful people. Best might be contributions that required a respondent's special understandings and abilities. What seemed important was that the activity be one that showed respondents that they still mattered to others.

Is it necessary still to matter to others, to have meaning in one's life? Can meaning in life be found just in being? There is something romantic in the idea of quiet self-sufficiency. Yet the respondent in our study who came closest to living a life of quiet self-sufficiency, a retired professional who spent winters alone in what had been his family's summer home, seemed when interviewed to be bitter at the direction his life had taken, even while insisting that he was doing just fine. He no longer had work, and he was for much of the time separated from family. His morning walks were taken alone; his afternoons, when he sometimes went shopping, might bring him in contact with others but not in a way that made a difference. The good books with which he had intended to spend his evenings turned out to be poor substitutes for company. It seems as if in later life, no less than earlier in our lives, we need to be part of things.

Older Americans may not be helped to remain part of things by the American tendency to define even the active members of the Third Age as no longer of social significance.

It appears to be in the American grain to value those able to act effectively: the gifted athlete, the young and energetic business leader, the attractive man or woman who can do it all. Aging suggests to us not the accretion of experience but rather a loss of edge, a slowing down. Our society has in it too few valued places that only those of retirement age can fill. We too little recognize that their years have made those in the Third Age repositories of our collective memories and that, from their confrontations with the inescapable crises of life, they have achieved some measure of wisdom.

The American attitude toward aging is neither necessary nor universal. As Gutmann points out in this book, in more traditional societies the aged can be respected teachers and guides. Insofar as those in the Third Age are treated by American society as socially irrelevant, it is a loss all around: not only would recognition of their potential contributions be of value to those in the Third Age, but it could greatly benefit the larger society.

But if it is important that we matter to others, it is also important that we make sense to ourselves. Becoming older can be bewildering, or dismaying, for someone for whom youthful vigor was essential or for whom it was important to have an open future full of possibilities. There may be questioning—how did I come to be here? Life review, as Rubinstein notes in this book, may not be the answer. The issue is not really making sense of the past; it's making sense of the present.

Several of our authors argue, and both Morris and Dobrof demonstrate, that what matters is remaining, at one's core, oneself. By the time someone has reached the Third Age, he or she will have witnessed any number of changes in the society, including changes in how people relate to each other and what people think is important. They may do best who take these changes in stride, changing and developing as is appropriate but throughout remaining themselves. The respondent in our interview study who had shifted from engineering to craftsmanship in wood changed his routine dramatically but became even more true to an unchanging inner core.

There is much work in social psychiatry to support belief in the importance to well-being of seeing life as meaningful. More and more of us are living to ages at which issues of meaning must be reconsidered from the vantage point of having now traveled much of the way. The meaningfulness of life is not reduced by entrance into the Third Age, but it may well newly require attention. The aim of this book is to help its readers better understand the issues involved.

ONE

Holding onto Meaning
through the Life Cycle

Peter Marris

EDITORS' INTRODUCTION Marris describes the
changes in our concerns as we move through life. In our
earliest years we attend first of all to our security and,
when our security has been established, to opportunity
for exploration. Our concerns then widen and become
more complex as childhood gives way to adolescence.
Adolescents ponder, among other things, the principles
according to which life should be lived; in adolescence
we begin questing after meaning. But during the long
years of adulthood that follow adolescence, with adulthood's responsibilities for self, home, and job, what matters is likely to be so obvious that there is no point in giving it attention. What matters is to make good on our
commitments: financial, parental, marital, social. When
adulthood gives way to later life, issues of meaning may
again arise.

   Despite the changes in our concerns, we remain
throughout our lives recognizably ourselves in the categories we use for understanding and in our assumptions
about ourselves and others. Even though the situations
of our lives change, our personalities, although they may
be modified as we adapt to new situations, have at their
core a continuous self. Indeed, as we move from the
years of working and raising children into later life we

may be surprised at the extent to which we feel ourselves to be unchanged in our core from our adolescent and early adult selves. And yet, in later life, there are many disruptions: the ending of work almost certainly, possibly geographical relocation, possibly bereavement. Should fundamental change occur, our prior ways of managing may lose their effectiveness, with the result that we experience confusion, dislocation, distress. As Marris says, a lifetime's investment in a way of seeing things can become a barrier to new learning.

Not all the changes that come with age are negative, and adaptation to the more positive changes may require little effort. Still, it can take a bit of time to become accustomed to freedom from the many concerns of earlier life. There may even be a bit of a sense of loss in finding oneself less concerned with establishing and maintaining a place in one's community, and less absorbed by worry over meeting the bills. But more troubling, as we move on through the Third Age, are losses: our careers are left behind, our physical capacities diminish, people die. Even in the absence of loss, relationships change, with friendships sometimes fading because of distance and depleted energies. If we are unlucky, we may encounter changes in ourselves: diminished energy, physical limitations, a sense of not being as effective as we once were.

Through all this change we try to make sense of what is happening. One aid to making sense of what is happening, to giving meaning to every part of our lives, is recognition that even as our lives themselves have a trajectory from childhood through age, our lives contribute to the immense trajectory of generations. We are a link between those who inhabited the world before our arrival and those who will inhabit it in the future.

To be sure, this recognition is only one way of providing meaning to our living and having lived. We can also find meaning in having met the challenges of our earlier and present lives. We can find meaning in our contribution to enterprises and institutions and causes. But recognition of our linkage to those who preceded us can help us understand how we came to be ourselves, and recognition of our linkage to those who follow can reassure us that our lives, however lived, have mattered to others. We have benefited from the efforts of those who preceded us and, if all has gone well, we have provided and continue to provide support and direction to our successors.

In the familiar stereotype, life is a progress from innovation to conservatism. The young rise to the challenge of change; in maturity we consolidate our understanding; in old age we become set in our ways. Yet the old must, and do, constantly adapt to changes, as much or more than the young or middle-aged, because their physical and social resources are less able to control the circumstances of their lives. Age differences are not, I suggest, differences in adaptability but in the historical experiences through which we have learned to adapt and in what we have to adapt to at each stage of life.

At any age, to assimilate change and respond to it, we must already possess a context by which it can be interpreted. We have to be able to categorize events before we can deal with them, and we cannot learn unless the categories are stable and consistent enough to sort experiences into cumulative knowledge. Over time, we elaborate and refine structures of meaning for all the classes of events and relationships we encounter. We become increasingly confident of these meaning structures as they successfully interpret more and more experiences. But to sustain this confidence, we must perceive the events we encounter selectively, ignore whatever is anomalous or contradictory, compartmentalize mutually incompatible ways of structuring experience, and avoid situations that would bewilder our understanding. We have to simplify and abstract in order to classify and generalize experience, because each event is unique and therefore open to a potentially disorienting variety of interpretation.

We can also, within limits, make the world fit our preconceptions, choosing relationships we understand and manipu-
lating them to conform to our expectations. This is our "assumptive world," as Colin Murray Parkes has called it—what
we believe we understand and have come to rely on as we live
our lives from day to day (Parkes, 1971; see also Marris, 1986).
The loss of this assumptive world is deeply threatening, even if
nothing outwardly has changed. Loss of faith, or loss of trust
in someone we love, can be as devastating as a bereavement.
At every stage of life, therefore, we seek to hold onto this assumptive world, and at every stage we may face crises when
the structures of meaning on which our understanding rests
threaten to disintegrate. What changes is not the impulse to
hold on to what we know and trust, or the struggle to reestab-
lish the sense of a meaningful life, but the nature of our vulnerability. We think of attachment to familiar ways, and an
unwillingness to test our preconceived ideas against new experiences, as characteristic of the conservatism of the old. But
these impulses are surely as powerful in our childhood and
youth.

Throughout childhood we continually enlarge our experience, master new skills, and learn how to manage new levels
of relationship. We are often hurt and bewildered, and even
the most supportive adults cannot clear up all our confusion
or rescue us from the ambiguities of love and conflict. Children tend to be fiercely conservative when their familiar bases
are threatened. Growth builds on what has been consolidated.
A one-year-old child, exploring a strange room, returns from
time to time to Mother and exchanges glances with her, re-
newing contact with the secure base from which to branch
out on new ventures. As John Bowlby wrote, "first the child,
then the adolescent and finally the young adult moves out in a
series of ever lengthening excursions. . . . Each step follows the
previous one in a series of easy stages. Though home ties may

be attenuated they are never broken" (Bowlby, 1970; see also Bowlby, 1988). The conservatism of childhood expresses itself through attachment to home, and so long as this is secure, children are confident in exploring new meanings and new relationships.

By contrast, the conservatism of adolescence may express itself through ideological rigidity. Richard Sennett (1970) has suggested that the adolescent search for identity can result in a perversion of learning, in that the defense of a theoretical understanding leads to the rejection of experience. Confronted with the choices that will determine their future, adolescents desperately need principles to guide them. They cannot wait for experience to inform their decisions and so must either make conventional, imitative choices or commit themselves to ideals they have not tested. The defense of these conceptions can become so important that no test of them is ever risked—hence the political idealist who rejects all political action as co-optive or the writer who waits forever for the moment of inspiration.

In adult life, the tension between keeping up and holding on becomes embodied in the more or less settled patterns of relationship that govern our lives—family, jobs, career. The choices are less open and the changes more costly. We become the generation in charge, and we discover that the relationships that govern social behavior—the conventions, laws, organizations, customs, and values—cannot be taken for granted but have constantly to be reproduced in the daily effort of living. Changing them can be profoundly threatening, if not to ourselves, then to others, because it could undermine the skills and sense of identity we have acquired through coping with things as they are. If we grow more cautious, it is partly because we come to realize that, despite our best efforts, anything, however secure it seems, can fall apart—a marriage, a business, a democratic system.

At the same time, since most adults, sooner or later, commit themselves to a marriage, a career, a country in which the meaning of their lives comes to be invested, the crisis of meaning is more profound should this structure of relationships collapse. And because love, self-respect, reward, and ambition are all bound up together in this structure, the collapse of any part of it can devastate the whole. Whenever we lose someone or something of central importance to us, all the activities that relate to that object lose their purpose. Everyday routines that used to occupy us, and whose fulfillment represented the constant rhythm of our lives, suddenly become pointless. The world about us begins to seem meaningless, too, because we are bereft of the purposes that organized it in a relevant way. A severe loss tends to undermine the meaning of other crucial relationships as well. If a man loses his wife, though his career is intact, he may wonder what he is working for now. Conversely, when plant closings rob workers of the jobs in which their self-respect and economic security have been invested, they may suffer emotional problems that put their marriages at risk (Kasl & Cobb, 1979). Widows in the critical phase of grief may not be able to feel the needs of their children as a sustaining reason to go on living (Marris, 1958). The crisis of meaning tends to become pervasive, so that the whole organization of reality from which the sense of life derived is undermined.

This crisis provokes grief. The process of grieving is essentially a difficult and painful search for a way to reconstruct a meaningful world, and it works itself out through the interplay of two contradictory impulses. At times the bereaved may try to recover the past—to relive memories and go on as if the lost relationship were still present. But when present reality intrudes again, they are only more painfully reminded of their loss. So at times they may, conversely, also try to escape into the future, to become a new person with new purposes, for whom the past can be forgotten. But this impulse, too, pro-vokes a reaction—a sense of betraying the lost relationship and all it meant. So each impulse tends to be self-limiting, urg-ing the griever back to confront the loss; and each represents one part of what is needed to reconstruct a meaningful life. The bereaved have to recover purposes, worthwhile to them, that the future can fulfill; but these purposes must grow out of the past experiences of love and purpose in which their capac-ity for emotional attachment is rooted. In the process of griev-ing, the past is consolidated: although the relationship is lost, its meaning is redefined and reasserted. Once it is possible to feel that the past cannot be snatched away, that its meaning is secure, the bereaved can begin to abstract from the relation-ship a meaning that can be reformulated to guide the present. As a widow works through her grief, for instance, she may at first act as if her husband is still alive—imagining herself talk-ing to him, reliving their experiences together, often, too, reas-suring herself about the quality of the relationship. As time goes by, she will speak of her husband more as a reference for present action—trying to think what he would have done or what he would have wished. Eventually, these purposes may become incorporated as an expression and extension of the ideals they shared, without explicit reference to him.

C. S. Lewis, in his autobiographical book *A Grief Observed* (1963), gives a vivid account of how the loss of his wife pro-voked a profound crisis of meaning, where his religious faith, his sense of his past, his whole sense of life at first disintegrate; and how, gradually, through the reassurance that he can recall his wife's presence, that she will continue to exist for him in recollection, he is able to abstract from their relationship an abiding, more generalized sense of spiritual communication that restores his faith. I am struck, especially, that his religious beliefs, though they were strongly held and the subject of his best-known books, disintegrated in the face of loss and that they did not support him in his grief. Later, the working-through of grief enabled him to recover his faith.

Several of the widows I spoke with in a London study had also repudiated their religion—disillusioned with a guarantee of the meaningfulness of life that had proved untrustworthy (Marris, 1958). Why did religion, in all these instances, provide no consolation? The rationalization of suffering, the idea of Heaven as a blissful home where the living and the dead will be reunited, the insistence on the meaningfulness of God's design, even when it seems to us unintelligible, are all central to the Christian tradition and would seem to offer both support and hope. But there is a vital distinction between doctrine and personal belief.

To understand the world, interpret what happens to us, and make sense of our daily lives, we make use of both public and personal structures of meaning. Public meanings, like law or science, are constructed out of assumptions and logical relationships that are independent of our personal experience or purposes. So they are invulnerable to the disintegration of personal meanings that can plunge the bereaved into such despair. (For a discussion of this distinction between public and personal meanings, see Marris, 1996, especially chapter 6, "Meanings in Public and Private.")

In modern Western democracies, the status of religion as a public meaning—as a doctrine whose truth is independent of the personal experiences of the believer—is ambiguous. Most Christian denominations claim to represent universal truths, but religious tolerance depends on them being treated instead as personal meanings. In the United States, for instance, religious belief is encouraged as an expression of personal spiritual awareness and moral integrity. But when evangelists have tried to challenge the teaching of evolutionary theory in schools, their claim that religion represents a public meaning has generally been rejected. The great majority of Americans do not believe that religious beliefs are public meanings equivalent to scientific theory.

If religious beliefs are part of the personal structure of meaning, then they are vulnerable to bereavement. The widows of my London study, for instance, felt betrayed by their religion because, I think, it had meant to them a general reassurance that life was fair and that there was a meaningful relationship between virtue and happiness. As one woman said, "Why should my husband be taken? He was in hospital with a lot of old men. . . . And they used to get well. They were all over sixty, and they had nobody. But my husband was a young man, and he died. Religion has to answer that" (Marris, 1958, p. 18).

I suggest, then, that in Western society we most characteristically take religion as an assortment of moral prescriptions, symbols, rituals, and exemplary stories drawn from the particular cultural tradition into which we were born, which we may use to express some aspects of our sense of social identity and, perhaps, of our sense of life's meaning. As such, religion is an aspect of the personal structure of meaning that has to be reintegrated and reformulated by the working-through of grief. And because religion has become a personal rather than public structure of meaning, most of the formal mourning rituals that used to articulate the stages of grief have fallen into disuse.

Grieving for loss is the most profoundly innovative learning we undertake in our adult lives. It requires the abandonment of familiar meanings and the reconstruction of a new organization of reality. It involves unlearning as well as learning— and while we learn confidently when we are secure, unlearning is always dangerous. But this progress from the loss or abandonment of familiar understandings, through a stage of ambivalence, often clouded by bitterness and despair, to the abstraction and reintegration of the essential meanings of the past in a new synthesis is essential to recovery from loss.

We are most likely to face this task as we approach old age, and the chances of suffering a deeply felt loss inevitably increase. Our parents die; old friends move away, or become ill, or die; we begin to leave our careers and our colleagues; our bodies begin to break down. I remember the bitterness, as well as wit, with which my aunt described the tag sale where she cast out her possessions when she and her husband moved south to their retirement home. In the preceding few months she had had to come to terms with the death of old friends, the sudden loss of sight in one eye, and the selling of her home. The strain of assimilating all these changes almost overwhelmed her. This is what, as we age, we must somehow take in—at once keeping up and holding on to the thread of continuity in which the richness of our lives is embedded.

What we lose, and how we lose it, still varies greatly with social class and gender. Peter Townsend's (1957) study of old people in a working-class district of London showed how retirement undermined the self-respect of men. Not only did they lose the status of wage earner, but they became rather childlike dependents on their wives. According to the custom of their community, they had been used to giving their wives a housekeeping allowance from their wages—often without her even knowing what those wages were. In retirement, they handed over the whole of their pension to their wives and received in return a little pocket money. The wife now controlled the family budget, and what she could give her husband was not enough for him to treat his former workmates to a drink. He tended to withdraw from his former circle of friends, just when he had a lot of time to fill and needed activities away from home. The wives did not encourage their husbands to help with the housework and found them in the way. So men who thought themselves still physically and mentally alert might be reduced to spending long hours on park benches or in public libraries, taking walks on trivial errands, too poor to pay for the amenities of sociability and a nuisance to their wives. In this way, one change—retirement—may resonate through every aspect of life, undermining its meaning.

For the middle class, retirement is usually less absolute and less pervasive in its effects. There are hobbies, the responsibilities of voluntary work, opportunities to keep in touch with a career. The economic consequences are not typically as drastic and the patterns of household management are less segregated than in the London community of Peter Townsend's study. In a Britain more prosperous than it was then, working-class and middle-class patterns of life resemble each other more. But economics, and the skills with which we identify our claim to respect and social value, still affect what retirement means to us. For the better-off, the crisis may come later, not at formal retirement but when physical handicaps force them to give up work they value.

For rich and poor, men and women alike, the characteristic experiences of later life are likely to include losses that disrupt the crucial organizing purposes of life. Few are fortunate enough to "die young at an advanced age" with the identity and purposes of their prime intact. Often, critical experiences cluster together: illness provokes retirement, retirement provokes a move, the move puts family and old friends at a distance, and in the midst of all this someone dear to us dies. But there may be twenty years of life ahead, or more, and if people are to enjoy a meaningful old age, they have to work through these crises, as the bereaved work through their grief. The losses of relationships, of physical powers, of status and income have to be accepted, and yet essential purposes have to be retained, reformulated, and reincorporated in a new organization of reality. And this must be achieved with fewer resources than one used to enjoy—with more circumscribed physical and social control.

The conventional ideology of old age, especially perhaps in

the United States, is very little help to people in working through these crises. Our culture tends to reinforce attitudes that, in the context of bereavement, could be seen as a morbid refusal to come to terms with loss. As I described earlier, loss characteristically provokes contradictory impulses: to resurrect the past and to abandon it altogether. In normal, successful grieving, each impulse is self-correcting and the interplay between them sustains the search for a viable reintegration (see Glick, Parkes, & Weiss, 1974; Parkes, 1972; Parkes & Weiss, 1983). But grief does not always lead to a resolution; there are morbid expressions of grief that represent a fixation on one or another of these impulses. The bereaved may mummify themselves in the past, retreating into a way of life still absorbed in the lost relationship (Gorer, 1965). Or they may plunge busily into a new life, whose hollowness betrays its failure to retrieve a real sense of purpose: the crisis is driven out of mind but not resolved. Conventional approaches to old age seem to me to encourage both these distortions of grieving.

Contemporary American culture tends to treat old age as if it were itself a meaningful identity, a defining characteristic to be used to segregate people. Institutionalizing old age not only emphasizes the break with the past but implies that the elderly are to find meaning in the fact of being old. Some of the hobbies, pastimes, and busy work often recommended to the elderly can come to resemble the hollow activities of those who cannot grieve. Old age is not a quality of character. Old Charlie is still the Charles who wrote passionate love letters, won a celebrated court case. Old Charlie's wife is still the woman who was top of her class and whose beautiful hair was the envy of her contemporaries. If the hair is now white and the court case relegated to a footnote in a legal textbook, that does not make them different people with a different conception of themselves and different attachments. It only obliges them to find new ways of being themselves.

If we confer senior citizenship as if it were a meaningful identity, we also act as if it should not exist at all, as if the ideal were to preserve a vigorous youth to the last, to defy aging and collude in silence over its inevitable encroachments. Popular American culture constantly promotes the drugs, hormones, diets, and exercise regimes designed to forestall or counteract the symptoms of aging. Some of this may be valuable, but if we think of aging only in terms of physical decline, it makes old age a lost battle and mummifies youth. The idea of aging as, say, growing wisdom or wealth of experience is foreign to our cultural preconceptions: we talk a lot about memory loss but very little about the cumulative value of what we are trying to remember.

How then are we to make sense of life in old age, without either denying the reality of aging or losing ourselves in the spurious identity of a senior citizen? How do we reinterpret the purposes and attachments of an active life, so as to inform a changing, and probably more restricted, range of available occupations? To most people, grandparenting means a great deal—partly, I suggest, because it links us to youth and growth in a relationship where we can be useful and brings us closer to our children. But it is also the relationship that most surely carries something of ourselves beyond our lifetime. For the same reason, most of us, I believe, want to recollect and preserve something of our life's experience, passing that knowledge on to the next generation. As grandparents and as members of our community, our memories, shared with the young, link generations, keeping unbroken the thread of continuity that gives human society a unique historical dimension. It can be important not only to the older generation to impart something of ourselves to the future but to the younger generation to be able to see more clearly who they are through their links to the past.

My uncle undertook to research our family history in his old age, and I am grateful to him for the insight it gave me into the middle-class English culture into which I was born. In the London borough where I used to live, a group of historians recorded the reminiscences of old people who grew up in the harsh poverty of the East End, publishing them as illustrated pamphlets that sold very well in the local bookshops (the Hackney People's Autobiography Series, Centerprise, London). What these memoirs contribute is not simply entertaining. History is a crucial part of present meanings. A society without a history would not be able to explain itself to itself, just as a person without a history has no identity. Old people have a unique insight into the past, because they have lived it. A sense of having something to contribute that matters, not only to oneself and one's generation but to future generations, is vital to a meaningful old age.

Of course the old are not—except by professional choice—historians, and their memories are not history. Their contribution to historical narrative is marginal, compared to the documents, statistics, letters, and newspaper reports on which historians largely rely. Memories are fallible and self-serving. As they are incorporated into the historical narrative, cross-examined and compared, the rememberer loses ownership of them. History, as a younger generation now interprets it, takes the past as the older generation lived and still remembers it and turns it into something alien. As sources of historical knowledge, old people are used but lose control of the meaning of what they give, and this, I think, often makes them ambivalent about entrusting their memories to the young. For old people, as for anyone younger, their most valuable contribution is their insight into the present. Not that old age necessarily makes us wiser, but the depth of experience—the ability to look back on a life where, for better or worse, many of the tasks are over, framing that experience with a sense of completion—makes for a different kind of perception.

Each of us confronts the crises of aging from a unique standpoint: the retirement that undermines one may be the opportunity for another. It is more useful to acknowledge the crises, and understand the process of reconstruction, than to recommend the form reconstruction should take. If people recognize depression, disorientation, aimlessness, and loss of self as natural consequences of a crisis in life, they can at least begin to confront it. The onset of old age is not a single crisis but a series of events that may only be cumulatively critical. If we understand the effort and stress of coming to terms with these changes, we can begin to look for ways to avoid compounding the stress. And it may be easier to make sense of being old once we acknowledge that we begin to age almost as soon as we are fully adult. Aging and dying are part of everyday life, and all our purposes are framed in the knowledge that nothing is immutable. Whatever we want to continue must constantly be retrieved from loss and reincorporated. In that sense, the wisdom of old age is the outcome of a succession of bereavements, some traumatic, some so attenuated that we were scarcely aware of them until we finally came to terms with them.

NOTE

This essay is based on an earlier version published in *International Journal of Aging and Human Development,* 9(2) (1978–1979): 127–135.

REFERENCES

Bowlby, J. (1970, September). *Self-reliance and some conditions which promote it.* Presentation at the Tavistock Clinic Jubilee, London.

Bowlby, J. (1988). *A secure base.* New York: Basic Books.

Glick, I. O., Parkes, C. M., & Weiss, R. S. (1974). *The first year of bereavement.* New York: Wiley.

Gorer, G. (1965). *Death, grief and mourning.* Garden City, NY: Doubleday.

Kasl, S., & Cobb, S. (1979). Some mental health consequences of plant closings. In L. Ferman & J. Gordus (Eds.), *Mental health and the economy.* Kalamazoo: W. E. Upjohn Institute.

Lewis, C. S. (1967). *A grief observed.* London: Faber.

Marris, P. (1958). *Widows and their families.* London: Routledge.

Marris, P. (1986). *Loss and change.* London: Routledge.

Marris, P. (1996). *The politics of uncertainty: Attachment in private and public life.* London: Routledge.

Parkes, C. M. (1971). Psycho-social transitions: A field for study. *Social Science and Medicine, 5,* 101–115.

Parkes, C. M. (1972). *Bereavement: Studies of grief in adult life.* London: Tavistock.

Parkes, C. M., & Weiss, R. S. (1983). *Recovery from bereavement.* New York: Basic Books.

Sennett, R. (1970). *The uses of disorder.* New York: Knopf.

Townsend, P. (1957). *The family life of old people.* London: Routledge.

TWO

The Third Age

Robert L. Rubinstein

EDITORS' INTRODUCTION Rubinstein focuses his attention on the interval of the Third Age, the span of years between retirement age and the advent of age-imposed limitations. This is a time when adequate resources, adequate health, and few responsibilities provide a context for self-fulfillment, freedom, and purposeful engagement. How long the Third Age lasts varies among individuals, but it is likely to last several years and can extend for two decades or even longer. To be sure, not everyone who is an appropriate age has the health and the financial security that make the Third Age's freedoms possible. But those who had stable careers, even in blue-collar work, are very likely to meet the financial requisites of Third Age membership.

Rubinstein notes that those entering the Third Age will find little guidance regarding the merits and deficiencies of alternative ways of designing their lives. The Third Age is still too new to have attracted the attention of the mythmakers and model-providers of our society: our dramatists, novelists, and filmmakers.

The Third Age makes available many alternative core commitments: continued work, perhaps in a new field, in a different role, or for fewer hours; unpaid work for institutions and causes; travel; golf; visits to the children and grandchildren; or just living quietly: staying at home, with occasional get-togethers with friends and kin. To quite an extent, Third Age people use their freedom to extend the way of life they had already established. One new emphasis in the lives of many of those in the Third Age is care of the self. People want to stay healthy, physically and mentally, both to postpone decline and also as a sort of abstract responsibility.

Rubinstein points out that we have little information regarding how much change occurs among those in the Third Age. There is little evidence to support the image of someone revising his life's direction after a period of taking stock. Continuity in the way life is lived seems much more likely. Nevertheless, there can be reassurance and enhanced self-confidence in finding it possible to do what one wants to do, even if what one wants to do is just more of what one has always done.

The territory of later life has changed dramatically in the past decade or two. The American geriatric stage is now inhabited by persons who are, in general, healthier, wealthier, and better educated than their predecessors and likely to live longer. They have thoroughly accepted the postmodern focus on the body, youthfulness, pleasure, and health. They may retire and later "unretire." They may reinvent working as part-time employment, or as personally fulfilling volunteerism, or as consultancies. They remain active through travel, other leisure-time pursuits, and other personally fulfilling activities.

For those with adequate resources, adequate health, and few responsibilities, this period provides a context for self-fulfillment, freedom, and purposeful engagement that is largely new in human history. It makes possible the ability to plan ahead for what one will do weeks, months, and even years from now. And it provides the benefits of having become old enough to enjoy relationships with marital partners, children, and old friends, without the worry and effort that one invested in their development.

The term "Third Age" has come to mean this portion of the life span: postcareer and post–familial responsibility (Laslett, 1991). It is a time of life after retirement and the departure of the children from the home but prior to the onset of chronic illness and terminal decline. Its characteristics have been made possible by increased longevity, better health, and an increased level of financial well-being among the cohort of the newly old. Central among these characteristics is the leisure time for the pursuit of new or long-latent interests, together with desired levels of sociability.

Those for whom the image of the Third Age more or less fits seem to embody Anthony Giddens's notion of a post-traditional life course in which self-development "extends into the core of the self." Giddens observed:

> Transitions in individuals' lives have always demanded psychic reorganization, something which was often ritualized in traditional cultures in the shape of rites de passage . . . . In the settings of modernity, by contrast, the altered self has to be explored and constructed as part of a reflexive process of connecting personal and social change. (1991, pp. 32–33)

The project of self-construction is fostered by the extension into later life of the ideology of active individualism. In later life, active individualism becomes focused on the self in a fashion both more passive and more narcissistic than was earlier permitted by commitment to goals and responsibilities.

This image of an active, gratifying Third Age implies a positive image of later life and a humanistic conception of individual capacity for growth and change. In the rhetoric of the 1980s, elders were pictured as mindlessly and selfishly seeking generous entitlements at the expense of others in the society. The active, self-realizing Third Ager provides a cultural image that countervails such negative images as that of the "greedy geezer."

The negative image of elders as leisured, monied, narcissis-tic hedonists, oblivious to the needs and fates of their children and grandchildren is, of course, unfair and largely untrue. For some years now we have been witnessing the biggest inter-generational transmission of assets from elders to juniors, through family transfers, in the history of the planet. Further-more, half of all elders, and especially women and minorities, are not at all well-off economically. About 20% of all elders live at or under 125% of the federal poverty line while another 20% or more, who live at or under twice the poverty level, are economically vulnerable to any unexpected major expense, such as might be produced by serious illness.

Our current idea of a Third Age is no more true for all those entering their later years than the notion of the greedy geezer that it is supplanting. There has as yet not been adequate ap-preciation of the fact that the Third Age is a club of sorts, with minimum health and financial entry criteria. In reality, many of those whose age, taken alone, would make them "Third Agers" continue to have family responsibilities, work loads, and financial woes. They are disqualified by their lack of disposable leisure time from membership in the category. Nor does membership in the Third Age seem appropriately granted to "couch potatoes" or to others unmotivated to use well their gift of time. Instead they might simply be classified, pejoratively, as people who are old.

We have a situation in which aging is increasingly contextu-alized; that is, is increasingly a different experience, depending on health, income, and decisions regarding continuation at work. There no longer is a single progression of steps from birth to death like those portrayed in the "Stages of Life" prints that were once widely distributed. Careers no longer necessarily follow the traditional patterns of long tenure with a corporate entity, followed by a definite period of retirement. Instead, they increasingly are self-managed in response to personal needs or, sometimes, are disrupted by such vicissitudes as midcareer job loss. There is indeed an interval that might justly be called a Third Age for many Americans but hardly for all.

Giving Meaning to Life in the Third Age

As Clifford Geertz has noted, humans live in webs of meaning they themselves have spun. Lack of meaning is usually a temporary state, analogous to lack of ability to narrate. Or it may derive from experiences so profound that no voice or mindset can be conjured for them (Scarry, 1989). These sources of lack of meaning must be distinguished from developmental ambiguity. It is this last that is a real possibility for the historically new Third Age.

The developmental ambiguity of the Third Age shows itself in the uncertain linkage of the Third Age to Erik Erikson's life stages. The Eriksonian issue of the Third Age should be generativity. On the one hand, it would appear that nothing about, say, playing golf is generative. But generativity may be given a larger meaning than Erikson gave it. It can mean not only a concern with parenting and grandparenting, with developing and guiding the next generation, but also, more globally, a concern with what will happen after one's death and the dissolution of the self. Thus generativity may be found in any activity—social, political, or cultural—that concerns itself with the settings in which one's children and grandchildren will live. Even engaging in such leisure activities as golf can be seen as modeling a still-active, enjoyment-seeking way of life for future generations.

The developmental ambiguity of the Third Age may be made the greater by the role of cohort identity in Third Age beliefs and values. Every cohort has a particular cultural orientation, set down early in its life, that has shaped its values, behaviors, and predilections. While there is no guarantee that earlier values will reemerge in the behaviors and concerns of those in the Third Age, a cohort raised on activism is likely to remain activist. And yet there is nothing that would prohibit a cohort, upon reaching the time of "freedom from," in its Third Age, from manifesting a new concern, such as spirituality, that is not incompatible with earlier values but that could not have been predicted from them.

Individual concerns, distinct from those of the cohort, may also emerge in the Third Age to provide a context of meaning. One possibility, for example, might occur around issues of postwidowhood dating in which an active and playful sexuality, absent from the earlier marriage, can be seen to emerge. This would not be a reversion to an earlier stage of life but rather a reworking of earlier emotional and self-image issues in the new stage of life. Or it may simply be the use in the new life stage of guidelines from "the last time I was free," as an informant in a discussion with me once put the matter. Or it may be a product of a new permissiveness toward the self within the context of a cohort-provided environment in which attention is focused on the body, health, sexuality, and relatedness.

Should the wider society begin to see those in the Third Age as engaging in hedonistic behaviors more appropriate to the young, there could arise a new polemical image of Third Agers analogous to that of the "greedy geezer" of an earlier decade. This might draw on the classic image of the oldest old as reverting to a second childhood and picture the Third Ager as having returned, in an unseemly and discomforting fashion, to a time of teenage self-indulgence. Within a culture based in Puritanism, this would constitute a dismaying inversion of appropriate life course development.

It may well be the case, though, that given freedom and the belief in their right to self indulgence, Third Agers may seek to realize dreams and fantasies they had earlier foregone. They may learn piano, hike the Rockies, or buy an apartment in Paris. Meaning, for them, would be sought in the realization of deeply felt wishes that had been put on hold in earlier life. Most, to be sure, would continue their lives as they have been, perhaps giving more time to household and leisure pursuits that had long been important to them, but not taking on anything new. But some may treat the Third Age's gift of freedom creatively and imaginatively, and use it to expand their sphere of experience.

In truth, however, we cannot be sure how people find contexts for meaning as they enter the Third Age. It seems unlikely that they would be able to extend the context of meaning that they used during the main segment of their adult lives into the Third Age. Their work, which would have been for many the determinative context for meaning, will have ended. They may, perhaps, seek the gratifications of work—a sense of usefulness, perhaps—through sports, travel, and hobbies. But we do not know.

To my knowledge, there have been very few studies of the inner process of symbolic reorganization in later life—of how meanings are modified or sloughed off as lives change. Although a few studies of widowhood, retirement, and illness have approached this issue, we have little general understanding. Nevertheless, it seems reasonable to suppose that earlier meanings are never lost. But how they are stored, and whether they are compartmentalized away, or somehow integrated when new meanings take center stage, has as yet been given too little attention.

One hypothesis regarding the development of meaning in the Third Age seems to me suspect. It seems to me unlikely that most people entering the Third Age consciously reconsider, reshape, and reintegrate earlier life meanings through a process of life review. Robert Butler (1963) initially proposed the life review as a natural part of aging, a precondition for successful end-of-life ego integration. Butler's suggestion that the life review is a natural part of aging has been highly influential (Coleman, 1986), and the literature on the life review has become vast and complex. Nevertheless, the life review as an entity is poorly theorized. There is often uncertainty about where normal reminiscence ends and the life review begins. Often the literature has conflated the two.

I believe that the life review is neither necessary for the transition into the later-life phase of the Third Age to be satisfactory nor likely to be triggered by that transition. Western folk beliefs often group aging, illness, and degeneration into a triune unity. I have heard many informants say, "I didn't feel old until I got sick." The identification of aging and illness is socially deleterious because it emphasizes the negative aspects of aging. But it also means that in the absence of disability it is unlikely that people will consider themselves truly old.

It appears to me that the life review, as a fairly focused and identifiable phenomenon, is triggered by events that threaten the self: chronic or acute illness, impending death, or whatever else might produce a profound sense of finitude. The hallmarks of the Third Age, in contrast, are freedom, wealth, and health. These are hardly the prompting conditions for the life review.

The onset of chronic illness may mark the end of the Third Age and the point at which the life review process may be triggered and one's life story reevaluated through reminiscence and identity construction. Illness is an occasion for narrative (Kleinman, 1989), and chronic illness provides an important context for self-interpretation, reevaluation, and meaning making. But for those in the Third Age, the future continues to be open and life review unrequired.

Modern Culture and the Future
of the Third Age

There is always a lag between a social development and the widespread adoption of a set of ideologies about it. The newness of the Third Age itself is responsible for many of the difficulties of meaning with which it is associated. Given the newness, those who may be in the Third Age face a number of uncertainties: regarding the extent to which the activities of earlier life should continue into the Third Age; regarding the legitimacy of exploration, in the Third Age, of wishes and desires repressed during the main portion of adult life; and, more generally, regarding plans for living. The newness is expressed in the questions asked by those who study the Third Age: When does it begin? When does it end? What are its essential characteristics? What other paths in aging are there, in addition to the path leading to and through the Third Age?

We have not yet seen the social processing of the changes associated with the Third Age. I am struck by the lack of attention in popular culture to the Third Age and to the young old in general. There are, to my knowledge, few novels, songs, television shows, or other cultural representations of this time of life. Most representations of the elderly in popular culture focus on people older than the Third Agers. From the perspective of popular culture, perhaps, Third Agers are just not that interesting. The period might be viewed as a kind of late latency, a transition between the more vital earlier period of work and childraising and the more quiescent period of later life and diminished independence.

The Third Age poses interesting and important issues regarding the balance between individualism and communalism that our culture will endorse. When viewed as a period of freedom from responsibility for others, the Third Age is a time when the concerns of the individual can be emphasized. This does not imply that Third Agers are poor citizens or poor comembers of communities. Rather, this is their time for themselves. When viewed as a period of freedom from insecurity, however, the Third Age can be seen as a time when people are free to be of service to others.

I have noted that, in Eriksonian terms, the Third Age can be seen as shaping the conflict between narcissism and generativity. Narcissistic choices will have been made possible by a developmental environment in which the needs and demands of others have been lifted, allowing the full expression of one's wishes for oneself. The Third Age is a time in late life in which individuals can celebrate their ability to do what they want and so experience the agency of their persons.

Generativity, as I have noted, can at this time take the form of concern for children and grandchildren. It can also take the form of concern for the larger community through volunteer work or even modeling for younger people the vitality that is possible to later life. Nevertheless, our culture nudges those in the Third Age toward the narcissistic. It does so largely by defining the individual as the locus of responsibility for whatever happens to the self.

Our culture teaches that people are responsible for their own self-maintenance. In the Third Age this pushes people toward medical awareness, proactive intervention, wellness techniques, the tactical use of exercise and diet, even cosmetic surgery to enhance appearance. As an extension of self-maintenance, those in the Third Age are pressed to cultivate their selves through learning, travel, and the seeking of new experiences. Because it is a responsibility to remain mentally active, Third Agers can feel it important to engage in new learning and to take gingko biloba and antioxidants or whatever other products are reputed to enhance cognition and memory.

Many older people will fail to answer the call of such an ideology. Some will not have the energy or desire and may be disparaged as couch potatoes. Others will have been ill, disabled, or poor at the time their work ended. These people may be seen as having moved from earlier adulthood directly to the Fourth Age.

Much of literature on the Third Age has defined it, as I have done, as a "post" experience. In consequence there has been little consideration of what comes after the Third Age. Third Agers themselves can, for a time, insulate themselves from awareness of the Fourth Age to come. Meanwhile they are in a time of life that is both old age and not old age. The meaning of this time must include concern with how long the period can last: how long it will be before it is ended by serious illness or death.

The Third Age is lived against a background of realization of what comes next. The meaning of any activity in the Third Age is colored by awareness of a powerfully ambiguous future. Those in the Third Age may ignore the coming darkness, but they may instead acknowledge the uncertain future and, perhaps, work to make peace with it. One way to make peace with the future would be to think of the present and past from the future's perspective and so to anticipate later reminiscence and life review. To do so would find meaning in the present by anticipating how it will be understood when one has gone beyond the Third Age.

REFERENCES

Butler, R. N. (1963). The life review: An interpretation of reminiscence in the aged. *Psychiatry, 26,* 65–76.

Coleman, P. G. (1986). *Ageing and reminiscence processes: Social and clinical implications.* Chichester, U.K.: Wiley.

Giddens, A. (1991). *Modernity and self-identity: Self and society in the later modern age*. Stanford, CA: Stanford University Press.

Kleinman, A. (1989). *The illness narratives: Suffering, healing and the human condition*. New York: Basic Books.

Laslett, P. (1991). *A fresh map of life: The emergence of the Third Age*. Cambridge: Harvard University Press.

Rubinstein, R. L. (1987). The significance of personal objects to older people. *Journal of Aging Studies, 1,* 225–237.

Scarry, E. (1989). *The body in pain: The making and unmaking of the world*. Oxford: Oxford University Press.

THREE

The Changing Meaning of Aging

Harry R. Moody

EDITORS' INTRODUCTION Moody explores the
meaning that is attributed to aging by the people who
speak for our society. Drawing on best-seller lists of popular and professional books, Moody reviews for us the
changing opinions of the postwar years. In the years im-
mediately following World War II, when the focus of the
nation was on a return to normalcy, the aged were seen
as a group vulnerable to disability and as a social problem. But then the historical situation changed. In the late
sixties and early seventies the institutions of the society
came into question. It was a time of, in Moody's terms,
public pessimism and private optimism. Community
became less important than self-realization. In the public
mind the aged were an interest group whose claims were
competitive with the claims of other interest groups,
including children. But then, in another shift, self-
realization came to be defined in less material terms.
New models appeared for those in later life that emphasized their potential for continued development and
activity. A good many books celebrated the vitality of
aged individuals who directed enterprises, traveled,
wrote, and painted. Some authors recommended spiritual journeying. This seems to be where we now are.

  After telling this story Moody steps back and asks why
we have not settled on a stable image of aging and the
aged. His answer, it would seem, is that aging has no

necessary meaning. Philosophers and psychologists have pointed to changes that aging brings to the way we understand our lives. Alone among living creatures, we not only live but know that we live, and know that the time of our lives is bounded. As we age we become increasingly aware of finality and increasingly engaged by the bewildering problem of making sense of a moment we know to be fleeting. Life can be deeply satisfying, even joyous, but even as we live, it slips through our fingers.

Early in our lives we can shrug off recognition of finality; so much time remains. In later life awareness of finality can present us with the nagging problem of how best to use the time we still have and how to make sense of its limitation. It may be that our society continually revises its definition of what it means to be old because so many of us are uncomfortable with the awareness that time holds us, ever so gently, ever so inexorably, within its grip.

Popular works about aging in the late twentieth century have reflected changing American ideas about the meaning of age, as we can see when we look at popular literature from the 1970s through the 1990s.

Popular books on aging in the 1970s fall broadly into two categories: social criticism and the psychology of midlife. On the social criticism side are two classics of gerontology: Robert Butler's Pulitzer Prize–winning book *Why Survive?* (1975) and Simone de Beauvoir's *Coming of Age* (trans. 1972). Both convey an overwhelmingly negative view of aging and construe the condition of the aged as a matter for urgent public action. Age is presented as a social problem, an item for remedial social intervention. Butler's book, in particular, is an example of a familiar genre of landmark works, others of which are Michael Harrington's book *The Other America* (1962), Rachel Carson's *Silent Spring* (1962), and Betty Friedan's *Feminine Mystique* (1963), books of the 1960s that launched significant social movements. Butler, who coined the term "ageism," is a member of this group of contemporary social critics. The link with feminist criticism is notable here. Before Simone de Beauvoir wrote *The Coming of Age* she had written the groundbreaking *Second Sex* (trans. 1953), and Betty Friedan, like de Beauvoir, would, as she herself aged, turn her attention to aging as a social problem.

Other than as a social problem, late life was given little attention. The 1970s were a time when books on midlife psychology attracted wide public interest. Preeminent here was Daniel Levinson's *Seasons of a Man's Life* (1978) along with its popularized version, Gail Sheehy's best-seller *Passages* (1976). Both Levinson and Sheehy seemed to presume an implicit formula: midlife equals growth, old age equals decline. In fact, for both Levinson and Sheehy, adult development is limited entirely to midlife: old age as such is absent from their treatment of the life course. Like other writers after them, Levinson and Sheehy invoked the idea of "midlife crisis" yet would have us think of the middle years in more positive terms as a time of growth. The downside of the equation of midlife with growth is that when later writers wanted to find positive meaning in old age, the best they could come up with was to baptize it as a "second middle age."

The neglect or disparagement of age in popular writing was consistent with academic gerontology as well as with the broader public mood of the 1970s. Gerontology textbooks of the period, such as the early editions of Robert Atchley's classic text (Atchley, 1972, 1977), reflect a clear "social problems" perspective on old age. The same approach was embodied in public policy: the expansions of the Older Americans Act and increases in Social Security reflected a shared presumption that the elderly are a needy and vulnerable group, worthy of public subsidy. This is the attitude Robert Binstock (e.g., 1983) called "compassionate ageism." As an ideology, it served to legitimate public policy from the mid-1960s through the 1970s. The aged were seen as "the worthy poor," and that framework for legitimizing old-age politics endured even when antipoverty appeals lost political credibility in the 1970s and 1980s.

We need to appreciate this link between negative popular images of old age as weak, dependent, vulnerable, and dependent and the shared consensus in favor of age-based entitlements. The evolution of ideas about the meaning of age cannot be separated from broader historical events of the period in question. The 1970s witnessed the Watergate scandal, the American defeat in Vietnam, steeply rising oil prices, a 50% fall in the stock market after 1973, and economic stagnation followed by hyperinflation. This turbulent background is essential to appreciating the appeal of self-help psychology. In a world where events were spinning out of control, it is not surprising that Baby Boomers just entering their thirties were attracted to the privatism of popular midlife psychology. With middle age not far ahead of them, Boomers needed hope of retaining some measure of personal optimism in an environment of decline. This, in sum, was the appeal of Sheehy's "map of adult life" in *Passages*. In an era of declining expectations, a philosophy of self-help called for each individual to find his or her own way through the shoals and boulders of the adult life course; books such as *Passages* offered a navigational chart. The result was a curious tension between public pessimism and private optimism that Christopher Lasch (1978) would call "the culture of narcissism" of the 1970s.

Over the next two decades, the duality between pessimism and optimism surrounding the meaning of age would reappear in different guises. In 1980, a time when America elected Ronald Reagan as its oldest president, pessimistic voices began crying doom about the future of an aging society. Reagan himself, however, preached unabashed optimism, promising both national revival and tax cuts. The realities of life proved uncooperative. Reagan's first term was punctuated by a full-blown crisis in Social Security financing. As the decade unfolded there were murmurs of "apocalyptic demography," the fear that America simply could not afford the aging society that appeared to be its future.

The 1980s saw the rise of the Generational Equity movement, which warned of conflict between age groups. Prophets of Generational Equity never achieved mass support, but they did prove influential among policy elites and the media. Their pessimistic mood echoed well into the 1990s, even at a time when federal budget surpluses and a booming economy should have diminished the force of their arguments. Despite the positive economic situation, public opinion polls showed that the public, especially younger people, had little confidence in the future of Social Security. The seasons of apocalyptic demography have borne fruit in shared public pessimism.

But countervailing private optimism was also running strong. Early in the 1990s appeared Ken Dychtwald and Joe Flower's *Age Wave* (1989), a book that pushed for positive images of aging precisely in response to looming demographic changes. To be sure, Dychtwald warned about bankruptcy through entitlement spending, but he also promised a "Gray Market" of unparalleled opportunity for business leaders. As the 1990s unfolded other popular works on aging picked up this optimistic theme in different ways, all of them transforming the meaning of age from failure to success. Betty Friedan's *Fountain of Age* (1993) continued Robert Butler's style of social criticism, but now individual activity was the key to growth. Lydia Bronte's *Longevity Factor* (1993) promoted late-life creativity, a theme echoed by Gail Sheehy's relentlessly upbeat *New Passages* (1995), which became a best-seller. In contrast to earlier ideas of predictable age-based transitions, in her new book Sheehy treated the entire life course as making possible limitless self-help and self-creation. Along the same lines, John Rowe and Robert Kahn's *Successful Aging* (1998) synthesized a decade of MacArthur Foundation–sponsored research that concluded that the meaning of age turns out to be the same as the meaning of midlife. Life simply goes on, though perhaps with more freedom of choice.

Still another approach to the meaning of age is found in books that identify aging as a spiritual journey. This idea of "Conscious Aging" was first announced at a 1992 Omega Institute conference under that label. A popular version of this notion appeared in Deepak Chopra's *Ageless Body, Timeless Mind* (1993), with its New Age denial of decline in later life. In a related vein Zalman Schachter's book *From Age-ing to Sage-ing* (1995) looked to what gerontologists call "decrement with compensation," where later life is a time for cultivating wisdom. Both Drew Leder's *Spiritual Passages* (1997) and my own *The Five Stages of the Soul* (1997) are eclectic treatments that locate the meaning of age in increased interiority and contemplation, a tendency that Bernice Neugarten, as well as Carl Jung, had earlier identified as a basic trend in the second half of life (see, e.g., Neugarten, 1976).

All these approaches to late-life development should be seen in conjunction with the background conditions of the 1990s. The decade was one of unprecedented economic prosperity (albeit unequally shared), nurtured by an ideology of privatism and tinged by elements of anxiety and spiritual restlessness. *Titanic,* a film depicting a disaster that befalls people enjoying extravagant material success—providing imagery for abundance punctuated by anxiety—became the blockbuster film of the decade. During the waning years of the twentieth century, in the midst of economic abundance, thoughtful Americans began expressing concern about the values and meanings of our common life. Whether Elderhostelers or graying Boomers, growing numbers began asking whether this was all there was to life.

Despite its treatment of the aged as constituting a social problem, the outlook of the 1950s had been overwhelmingly optimistic. The early years of that decade had seen the publication of Norman Vincent Peale's *Power of Positive Thinking* (1952) and Erik Erikson's *Childhood and Society* (1950). Just as Peale put a positive spin on traditional Christianity, so Erikson gave an optimistic reworking of Freud's pessimistic psychoanalytic thought. Instead of sin and psychic conflict, Peale and Erikson, each in his own way, offered Americans an ideology of hope and personal growth. "Progress is our most important product," announced Ronald Reagan each week when he served as host of *General Electric Theater* on television.

In the 1990s the same upbeat mood of self-help was apparent in books of the New Age variety, such as Marianne Williamson's *Return to Love* (1992), as well as in James Redfield's *Celestine Prophecy* (1993). The popularity of Sarah Ban Breathnach's *Simple Abundance* (1995) and Thomas Moore's *Care of the Soul* (1992) points to a craving among Americans for inspiration in "everyday spirituality." The self-help impulse is never far from the American mind, as may be especially evident today, when a never-ending "legitimation crisis" calls external authority into question. Andrew Weil's *Spontaneous Healing* (1995) echoes nineteenth-century American traditions (Christian Science, New Thought) with their optimistic belief in the power of positive thinking to change the world. Indeed, when it comes to aging, the granddaddy of all self-help books is *Life Begins at Forty* (Pitkin, 1932), dating from the same Depression era that gave birth to Alcoholics Anonymous. Twelve-step programs and denial of limits in age are close cousins.

This mood of spiritual self-help is understandable as the century and the millennium both draw to a close. Seen in the perspective of American history, the 1990s have been a decade preoccupied with an uncertain image of the future. At the beginning of the 1990s downsizing in corporate America caused widespread uncertainty, and by the end of the decade volatility in the stock market accentuated the mood. Personal economic insecurity both reflects and intensifies an ideology of privatism and global competition. A global economic order means that events in Indonesia or Japan can alter our individual expectations about the future. Doubts about global warming or the future of Social Security remind us of the limits of all expectations, to which the mood of self-help is one response.

Along with broader economic trends, a powerful demographic current is beginning to affect public ideas about the meaning of age. Each year four million Baby Boomers are turning fifty. Most hold views of human development that are broadly optimistic, but more and more are searching for guidance on matters of personal growth. Just as Dr. Spock offered a road map for boomer children in the 1950s, so there is a growing demand for guidebooks providing direction to aging Americans in the twenty-first century for spirituality as well as financial planning. Our image of the future, both personal and collective, is contradictory, open-ended, often dizzying. The meaning of age is a question at once intensely personal yet now experienced by millions of people. Yet the cultural resources available for a map of life are increasingly fragmented, nonexistent, or contradictory. Personal optimism and public pessimism weaken the connection between the subjective experience and understanding of the society. We continue to search for the meaning of our lives and, within that context, for the meaning of age.

Life review, self-knowledge, affirmation of meaning: these three terms form an attractive triad that can evoke so much in us. Together they constitute a tantalizing promise of fruition, completeness, and totality. They seem to offer a kind of Promised Land of identity of being and consciousness, crowned with words that echo Erik Erikson's celebrated definition of ego-integrity: "I am satisfied with the course my life has taken." Don't we all want to be able to announce these words of triumph at the end of our lives?

Yet there is much to question about the realizability of this hope. There is a tragic element in retrospection. Hegel had that in mind when he invoked the image of the Owl of Minerva at dusk. We get wisdom too late for it to do us any good. Hegel's aphorism is wholly consistent with Greek tragedy. Think of Oedipus at Colonnus: he gains a kind of redemption, but only when his life is over, when knowledge can no longer be put to any use.

Hegel's archcritic Søren Kierkegaard would suggest something even worse. Kierkegaard (1992) wrote: "We live life forward but understand it backward." The logic of retrospective meaning is exactly the sort of evasion that existential philosophers would call "bad faith." To live life forward, at any age, means to be poised on a knife edge of uncertainty. This is the reason why T. S. Eliot in the *Four Quartets* (1943) ridiculed the "wisdom of age" and rejected every kind of retrospective meaning, including much that we would call "life review" and applaud as a vehicle for "life satisfaction." In place of any retrospective meaning, Kierkegaard would find more solace in Jung's thoroughly Socratic concluding lines: "The older I have become, the less I have understood or had insight into or known about myself" (1963, p. 359).

This Socratic or existential turn brings us closer to the predicament faced by gerontology as we labor to find positive affirmations about old age, a temptation that is almost an occupational disease of gerontology. Our problem is that we are confronted with an almost irresistible temptation to follow the logic of retrospective meaning toward its conclusion. Is this not the reason why gerontology as a field is so persistently attracted to the idea of life review as described by Robert Butler and ego-integrity as defined by Erik Erikson? The absolute power of retrospective meaning—life review—constitutes one answer given by a secular world that cannot completely banish a spiritual hunger for meaning in the last stage of life. Unlike Kierkegaard, we are reluctant to embrace religious language, though we may occasionally bow in the direction of "spiritual" concerns. Isn't the framework of ego-integrity and life review the structure we must inevitably create in our search for meaning in old age once we have foregone religious faith?

Jung, as the outcome of his struggle with the issue of the meaning to be found in life, and in later life, could only offer the hope that meaning could somehow be found. And yet he could only, at the end, accept the "wisdom of unknowing," in which he recognized that self-knowledge, despite having all of one's past laid out before one, is elusive—perhaps, in a way that would be complete and integrated, impossible.

I want to suggest that this mood of tentative anxiety and agnosticism about self-knowledge represents what we might call, in a phrase from the film *Star Wars,* the "dark side of the force" in the search for meaning in later life. The dark side is, admittedly, a negative moment, a revelation of uncertainty and doubt: the fear that we may come up short, even come up empty at the last moment of life. But we need to hold on to this dark side, to use what Hegel called "the tremendous power of the negative."

The dark side of the force is all around us: in nursing homes, intensive care units, even in wrinkles half-glimpsed in the morning mirror. If we try to evade this dark side, we risk being ambushed by it and destroyed. And yet our civilization encourages us to look away. It encourages our monumental failure of nerve in the face of finality.

We cannot resist imputing some special meaning to the last stage of life, just as we do to other stages of life. The result is a condition of denial and repression of doubt about meaning.

We have, alas, slipped into a one-sided stance in this attitude toward meaning and aging, and this one-sidedness manifests itself in insidious ways: sentimentality, hyperactivity, secret despair, and, above all, unrelenting efforts to escape from facing the possibility that what Jung called "the forces of meaninglessness" will gain the upper hand. All these maneuvers represent the pervasive power of denial, the belief that we can eradicate the pathogenic force of doubt just as we hope to eradicate epidemic diseases. And when the day comes when we discover that these pathogens are still with us, perhaps have grown stronger, then we feel only astonishment and despair: "It wasn't supposed to be this way."

The modern predicament of finding meaning in old age comes about because, in many respects, we have been granted our fondest wishes. Just as in the fairy tale, to be given magic fulfillment of a wish is not necessarily to become happy. So, on the one hand, long life represents a projection of our wish to be happy on earth; on the other hand, aging and death threaten all that we find precious in a lifetime of love and accomplishment. No one has expressed the paradox better than Ernest Becker in *The Denial of Death:*

> Man is a worm and food for worms. This is the paradox: he
> is out of nature and hopelessly in it; he is dual, up in the
> stars and yet housed in a heart-pumping, breath-gasping
> body that once belonged to fish and still carries the gill-
> marks to prove it. His body is a material fleshy casing that is
> alien to him in many ways—the strangest and most repug-
> nant way being that it aches and bleeds and will decay and
> die. Man is literally split in two: he has an awareness of his
> own splendid uniqueness in that he sticks out of nature
> with a towering majesty, and yet he goes back into the
> ground a few feet in order blindly and dumbly to rot and
> disappear forever. It is a terrifying dilemma to be in and to
> have to work with. (1973, p. 26)

Becker wrote those words in 1973, and his remarkable book went on to win a Pulitzer Prize. But as if to remind us always to be cautious about fairy tales with a happy ending, Becker himself would tragically be dead only a short while after winning the prize.

REFERENCES

Atchley, R. C. (1972). *The social forces in later life: An introduction to social gerontology.* Belmont, CA: Wadsworth.

Atchley, R. C. (1977). *The social forces in later life: An introduction to social gerontology* (2nd ed.). Belmont, CA: Wadsworth.

Ban Breathnach, S. (1995). *Simple abundance: A daybook of comfort and joy.* New York: Warner Books.

Becker, E. (1973). *The denial of death.* New York: Free Press.

Binstock, R. H. (1983). The aged as scapegoat. *The Gerontologist, 23*(2), 136–143.

Bronte, L. (1993). *The longevity factor: The new reality of long careers and how it can lead to richer lives.* New York: HarperCollins.

Butler, R. N. (1975). *Why survive?: Being old in America.* New York: Harper & Row.

Carson, R. (1962). *Silent spring.* Boston: Houghton Mifflin.

Chopra, D. (1993). *Ageless body, timeless mind: The quantum alternative to growing old.* New York: Harmony Books.

de Beauvoir, S. (1953). *The second sex* (H. M. Parshly, Trans.). New York: Knopf. (Original work published 1949)

de Beauvoir, S. (1972). *The coming of age* (P. O'Brian, Trans.). New York: Putnam. (Original work published 1949)

Dychtwald, K., & Flower, J. (1989). *Age wave: The challenges and opportunities of an aging America.* Los Angeles: Tarcher.

Eliot, T. S. (1943). *Four quartets.* New York: Harcourt, Brace.

Erikson, E. H. (1950). *Childhood and society.* New York: Norton.

Friedan, B. (1963). *The feminine mystique.* New York: Norton.

Friedan, B. (1993). *The fountain of age.* New York: Simon & Schuster.

Harrington, M. (1962). *The other America: Poverty in the United States.* New York: Macmillan.

Jung, C. G. (1963). *Memories, dreams, reflections* (R. Winston & C. Winston, Trans.). New York: Pantheon. (Original work published 1962)

Kierkegaard, S. (1992). *Concluding unscientific postscript to philosophical fragments* (H. V. Hong & E. H. Hong, Ed. & Trans.). Princeton, NJ: Princeton University Press. (Original work published 1846)

Lasch, C. (1978). *The culture of narcissism: American life in an age of diminishing expectations.* New York: Norton.

Leder, D. (1997). *Spiritual passages: Embracing life's sacred journey.* Los Angeles: Tarcher.

Levinson, D. J. (1978). *Seasons of a man's life.* New York: Knopf.

Moody, H. R. (1997). *The five stages of the soul: Charting the spiritual passages that shape our lives.* New York: Anchor Books.

Moore, T. (1992). *Care of the soul: A guide for cultivating depth and sacredness in everyday life.* New York: HarperCollins.

Neugarten, B. L. (1976). Adaptation and life cycle. *Counseling Psychologist, 6*(1), 16–20.

Peale, N. V. (1952). *The power of positive thinking.* Englewood Cliffs, NJ: Prentice Hall.

Pitkin, Walter B. (1932). *Life begins at forty.* New York: McGraw-Hill.

Redfield, J. (1993). *The celestine prophecy: An adventure.* New York: Warner Books.

Rowe, J., & Kahn, R. (1998). *Successful aging.* New York: Pantheon Books.

Schachter, Z. (1995). *From age-ing to sage-ing: A profound new vision of growing older.* New York: Warner Books.

Sheehy, G. (1976). *Passages: Predictable crises of adult life.* New York: Dutton.

Sheehy, G. (1995). *New passages: Mapping your life across time.* New York: Random House.

Weil, A. (1995). *Spontaneous healing: How to discover and enhance your body's natural ability to maintain and heal itself.* New York: Knopf.

Williamson, M. (1992). *A return to love: Reflections on the principles of a course in miracles.* New York: HarperCollins.

FOUR

Social Sources of Meaning in Later Life

Richard A. Settersten, Jr.

EDITORS' INTRODUCTION Settersten approaches the issue of meaning in the Third Age by examining the extensive literature on the determinants of our values and our goals. There are, of course, many influences, but most important may be those we experience as we participate in our social worlds. We make sense to ourselves as we seek to make sense to others. We feel secure in our ability to make a difference as we witness our effectiveness. We also evaluate ourselves partly on the basis of others' evaluations of us. We are likely to lose confidence in ourselves should we see ourselves being treated as marginal and irrelevant.

Settersten considers how our connections to others give point to our daily existence throughout our lives. In the Third Age, as at other times of life, our dominant concerns are apt to be relational: we try to maintain our own emotional well-being through interaction with others, and we worry about the emotional well-being of those close to us. Yet our relationships are likely to undergo change. Siblings whose paths had, through adulthood, diverged from our own, become more a part of ongoing life. Our friendships change: we have fewer work-related friendships, perhaps fewer friendships overall, but a new appreciation of friendships of long standing. Our marital and familial relationships absorb more of our time and energy.

Our ability to act effectively as a person in the Third Age depends on the roles and responsibilities our social world makes available to us in our postretirement years. It also depends on the state of our physical, emotional, and social resources. If all goes well we will remain vital participants in the world around us, despite having moved on from the responsibilities of earlier life. If all does not go well, we will want at the very least to function independently. Many of us find intolerable the idea of becoming the responsibility of others, controlled by their routines and provided only with what they decide is good for us.

Rubinstein, in the preceding chapter, questioned the importance of life review in the Third Age. But even without full-scale life reviews, many of those in the Third Age will consider what their lives have been about. They may look back on a struggle for self-realization or on a series of challenges encountered and perhaps mastered. Some will see their lives to have been justified by achievements; others, by children; and still others will take pride in having lived lives during which, each day, they met that day's bills.

Most in the Third Age may not give a great deal of thought to what gives meaning to their lives. Nevertheless, the values and goals they express in their behavior, the things they have done that please them, and the activities they currently pursue together constitute a statement of what they find meaningful. As Settersten shows, many factors have gone into determining just what that is.

Questions about the purpose and meaning of human existence have been asked since the beginning of recorded history: What is the point in our being alive? And how can one live a life that is meaningful and fulfilling? A search for answers to these questions seems deeply rooted in human nature (see Wong & Fry, 1998).

The search for answers becomes particularly important in

later life. At this time, individuals may try to integrate their past and present experiences into a continuous, coherent, and meaningful life story that makes sense of the lives they have lived (Erikson, 1963). This task may become more urgent in the face of age-related declines and losses and the recognition that the end of life is approaching.

Personal goals and decisions are central to the creation of personal meaning, and the larger the goal or decision, the greater its influence (Little, 1998; Maddi, 1998). Of course, developmental goals are shaped by biological, psychological, and social capacities and constraints (Heckhausen, 1999; Settersten, 1999). These factors significantly reduce the range of potential options available to an individual at any given point in time; and they canalize (make more selective) the life course over time. This can be interpreted in positive or negative ways. On the one hand, the process of canalization, in restricting the number of possible developmental pathways, keeps the individual focused on specific tracks and may help to maximize his or her developmental gains (e.g., to reap the accumulated rewards of his or her skills and resources). On the other hand, constraints of these types, particularly those that are the result of social forces, might be considered negative, even oppressive, as entire classes of individuals are systematically denied certain opportunities or are placed onto negative pathways with little or no chance to leave them.

Meaning in later life must be considered from the vantage points of both human agency and social structure. It must consider the degree to which individuals actively create their own lives through the goals they set and the effort they expend to reach them. At the same time, it must consider the degree to which individuals' lives are determined by their place in the social structure. The circumstances in which individuals find themselves are not entirely of their own doing: processes of social selection sift and sort people into and out of various contexts (Clausen, 1995). Such factors can constrain or promote opportunities in powerful ways.

The task of understanding meaning in later life is important and difficult. A variety of frames of reference must be invoked, including those of the psychologist and sociologist, the theologian, and the people whose outlook we hope to understand. We need to learn what leads to lives that feel vital, realized, and meaningful or lives that feel empty and pointless. Only with such understanding can we evaluate the human worth of the economic, medical, scientific, and social successes that have led to our increased life spans.

Distant Social Contexts as Sources of Meaning

Culture

Culture structures the ways lives are lived, represented, and assigned meanings. Project A. G. E. (Age, Generation, and Experience) is the only study of which I am aware that has undertaken explicit comparisons of cultural frameworks that relate to the experience of old age. It has explored the meanings of aging within seven communities in four countries: Hong Kong, China; Swarthmore, Pennsylvania; Momence, Illinois; Blessington, Ireland; Clifden, Ireland; the Herero of Botswana; and the !Kung Bushmen of Botswana (Keith et al., 1994). In each site the investigators asked what age categories were used and how the categories were defined and expressed. They also asked how age categories were evaluated, how people of different ages were expected to participate socially, and how people of different ages actually did participate.

People in all seven sites found old age to be the least desirable time in life. The sites in the United States and Ireland reported the least negative reactions to old age, especially from older people themselves. However, responses were generally hedged by an important "If": "If you have your health." The most negative reactions to old age were found in the two African sites, presumably because life in those communities is significantly tied to health and vigor and aging regularly brings loss in physical abilities. Health status, along with material security, was everywhere thought to be the most important determinant of the quality of later life.

These findings are consistent with other research that shows that older people's perceptions of their health and the health of others affects how they understand the process of aging (e.g., Eisenhandler, 1989). Concerns about health and health-related statuses begin to emerge at midlife but become increasingly important for self-definition in the later years (Freund & Smith, 1997). Most older people hope and try to maintain their health. For many, growing old is defined by, and is a process of adapting to, declines in physical health. They do not feel old unless they are physically ill or depressed. This feeling may be exacerbated in cultures that strongly disparage dependence in old age. An older adult who can no longer control his or her bodily functioning is likely to be demoted to the status of "nonperson," a status often shared with children (Hockey & James, 1993).

In Project A.G.E., concerns about dependence and independence in old age were often expressed in Hong Kong, in the United States, and among the Herero. For Americans, being dependent on others was one of the worst of the changes that may come with old age. For the Chinese and Herero, on the other hand, dependence on others was one of the potentially good things about old age. For the Herero, one of the best things about being young is having responsibility for the care of elders.

Project A.G.E. found significant variation in the extent to which age is a basis for social separation. The American sites and the !Kung Bushman site constituted extremes. Among the !Kung it was difficult to find any situation in which people of only one age category were present. Instead, "people of all ages worked, rested, played, and ate together—often touching and leaning on each other" (Keith, 1994, p. 210). On the other hand, in the United States, and especially in the Swarthmore site, age defined many tight social boundaries, with "fine age distinctions" sorting people into age-graded social contexts.

Though its degree varies, an age-differentiated life course is common in most modern societies (Keith et al., 1994; Riley & Riley, 1994; Settersten, 1997). In an age-differentiated life course, social roles and activities are allocated on the basis of age or life stage. In what has been called the "tripartition of the life course" (Kohli, 1986), the life course is rigidly segmented into three separate periods of education, work, and leisure. This model takes work to be the central dimension that organizes life. As Matilda Riley and John Riley (1994) note, such a structure is convenient in that it creates orderliness in the entry into important social roles and activities and also in the exit from them. At the same time, however, a rigid tripartite structure restricts opportunities for various types of activity to specific periods of life. It may be that a society would use the talents of its population most effectively if it softened or even departed from such a structure, so that within it everyone, of every age, could participate in the mix of education, work, and leisure that was most suitable and desirable.

Cohort

Cohort experiences —those experiences shared by members of a society who are born more or less in the same year—may well contribute unique understandings to the nature of aging. The kinds of opportunities and expectations individuals have in all areas of their lives are conditioned by the times in which they live. These historical conditions therefore shape and set the parameters of life's meanings. In the United States, contemporary cohorts of older adults have witnessed both rapid and dramatic social change in their lifetimes. The elders of our time have experienced the Great Depression, World War II, postwar economic growth, the Korean War and the McCarthy era, dramatic changes in transportation and technology, the overthrow of political regimes, new recognition of civil rights, and fundamental transformations of sexual mores. The very oldest have lived through World War I and knew a time when women had no legal right to vote.

We also know that contemporary cohorts of older adults place great value on their religious and spiritual beliefs and exhibit high levels of religious and spiritual activity (McFadden, 1996). Indeed, Paul Wong (1998) has noted that current cohorts of older people find in religion a major source of meaning. Indeed, their churches may be their most important sources of support, other than their families (Koenig, Smiley, & Gonzales, 1988). For future cohorts, however, the importance of religion and religious institutions seems uncertain. It may be that individuals become more religious and spiritual as they age, moving away from the more materialistic and pragmatic outlook of their earlier lives toward an outlook that is more cosmic and transcendent (Tornstam, 1997). But it also may be that the high degree of religiosity and spirituality now evidenced among older people will be true only for this cohort. This cohort may have lived during a time now passing, in which religion was highly valued and individuals and families exhibited a high rate of participation in religious institutions. In any event, religious and spiritual activities and beliefs serve to create meaning and purpose in life (McFadden, 1996, p. 172).

Still, while contemporary elders encountered a common set of historical events and periods of social change, we cannot assume that their actual experiences were the same. Within the current cohort of older people there is significant variability across finer cohort divisions. The youngest were infants or toddlers at the onset of the Great Depression, while the oldest were in their late twenties or early thirties. Similarly, the youngest were too young to have served in the armed forces during World War II, while those even somewhat older may well have had significant military experience. In addition, even those who share precisely the same birth year may have had different experiences depending on sex, race, the social class of their family of origin, the region of the country in which they lived, and the values and belief systems of their families.

Demographic Change

Historical shifts in the key demographic parameters—particularly mortality, morbidity, and fertility—have created new "time budgets of adulthood," to use Gunhild Hagestad's (1990) phrase. These, too, affect life's meanings. We now have more, and healthier, years to spend in various roles and activities. As a result, roles and activities may be prolonged and their time schedules loosened. The sequencing of roles and activities may become more varied, and their structure may become more complex. The result may be a more flexible life course (Riley, 1985; Settersten & Lovegreen, 1998; Sørensen, 1991) in which age is less important in determining social roles and life experiences.

There has been much speculation about the way changes in demographic parameters may affect a society. For example,

Alice Rossi (1986) has argued that an aging population, because it is heavily female, brings the potential for a more humane and caring society. This argument, however, assumes that (1) as the age pyramid becomes more top-heavy, the values and concerns of older women will play a larger role in social thought, (2) the values and concerns of older women are more or less uniform, and (3) women's values are naturally more humane and caring than those of men. Other speculation emphasizes the new potentials associated with increased lifetime, including the possibility that individuals not only will arrive at old age feeling more fulfilled but will live their later years in more satisfying and meaningful ways. However, increased life expectancy may bring with it challenges and even problems for individuals, families, social institutions, and society at large. Bernice Neugarten (1995) has speculated about the costs of survivorship for those individuals who outlive spouses or partners, siblings, friends, and even children. Are their later years therefore destined to be lonely ones? Another question is the extent to which frailty and disability may mark the additional years of life. Have we added years to life without adding life to those years? There have been debates about the personal and social costs that may accompany gains in life expectancy and the larger numbers of older people that will result. These include controversies surrounding proposals to ration expensive life-saving medical procedures as a function of age (e.g., Callahan, 1987) and to reallocate government funds away from old-age programs and services and toward those that pertain to children (e.g., Preston, 1984).

I have thus far focused on rather distant social contexts as sources of meaning in the later years. I now turn to the more proximate social contexts in which central life experiences take place, such as family life, friendships and their networks, work, school, neighborhood, and the informal associations associated with leisure activities and volunteering.

Proximate Social Contexts
as Sources of Meaning

Work and Education

An individual's adjustment to the end of the work role will largely depend on whether work held much meaning before retirement. As John Kelly (1993) notes, identities of ability and worth persist even after the ending of actual work. Still, to the extent that the retired person's identity is tied to actually working, retirement may present a challenge (Gradman, 1994).

Most contemporary research suggests that by and large men make the transition to retirement without unhappiness or maladjustment (e.g., Reitzes, Mutran, & Fernandez, 1996). For women, the evidence is less clear, perhaps because it is often illness of the spouse or the self that encourages retirement (Szinovacz & Washo, 1992) or because retirement diminishes financial security, especially for women who are on their own (Guy & Erdner, 1993).

Many working adults indicate that they hope to continue to work beyond the usual retirement age, and many retired adults indicate that they would like to work and are capable of doing so (McNaught, Barth, & Henderson, 1991; Quinn & Burkhauser, 1994). Nevertheless, the last few decades have brought a worldwide shift toward earlier and earlier retirement (Kohli, 1994). Although some evidence suggests that these trends are now beginning to taper off (Burkhauser & Quinn, 1994), most workers, young and old, want to retain the option of retiring at the age now usual in their occupations (Rix, 1998). However, many find value in alternatives to moving directly from work to full retirement, such as bridge jobs, part-time work, and limited-time returns to work during retirement.

Some older people have replaced the structure and engagement of work with participation in adult educational programs oriented toward the older learner (Manheimer, 1998;

Manheimer, Snodgrass, & Moskow-McKenzie, 1995). Such programs are administered through senior centers, extension schools, vocational schools, community colleges, and four-year colleges and universities and may include students in teaching, institutional governance, and the development of curricula. Programs such as these not only increase the potential for "life-long learning" but also make it possible for individuals to resume and achieve educational or occupational goals they were not able to meet earlier in their lives.

Leisure and Volunteer Activity

The activities in which individuals are engaged constitute something more than simply "keeping busy"; they often express and reflect one's central values and hold important meanings (Kaufman, 1993). Volunteer activities, in particular, have been found to bring new meaning to the lives of men and women at midlife and beyond by permitting them not only to perform useful services but also to function as mentors, guides, and repositories of experience for those who are younger (Kleiber & Ray, 1993). Engaging in productive leisure activities also facilitates older people's well-being (Herzog, Franks, Markus, & Holmberg, 1998).

More than a quarter of older Americans perform volunteer work (Caro & Bass, 1995), and even more would do so if they had the opportunity (Cutler & Hendricks, 1990). The volunteer work is primarily done for religious institutions and organizations but also for hospitals, nursing homes, and hospice organizations. Participation in advocacy organizations, including political organizations, also serves as an important source of meaning in later life. The fact that older people display high voting rates is an expression of the importance to them of political developments (Binstock & Day, 1996; Torres-Gil, 1992; Wallace, Williamson, Lung, & Powell, 1991).

It seems to be the younger and healthier among the elderly who are most likely to participate in satisfying leisure activities (Johnson & Barer, 1992). Those who are older and less healthy are more likely to disengage from the wider social sphere of advocacy and volunteering and to move to a world of much-reduced scope. Still, among those who disengage to a world in which introspection in good part replaces social engagement, many seem content simply to take their lives day by day.

Personal Relationships

No one moves through life alone. An individual life is intimately connected to the lives of many others, and an individual's development is bound to, and shaped by, interaction with others (Elder, 1998; Settersten, 1999). Intimate ties in later life, like those earlier in life, shape one's experiences and life's meanings. Interdependence can affect decision-making. People whose lives are linked generally attempt to navigate life together; for example, husbands and wives may jointly coordinate the timing of their respective retirements so that they can spend more time together.

At the same time, interdependence can bring with it great unpredictability, in that a change in the life of one person requires adjustment in the lives of others, thereby creating asynchrony. When lives are asynchronous, relationships may be strained. For example, the serious illness of a parent, spouse, or child may create an unexpected need to provide care, may require immediate accommodations in work and other activities, or may even bring the need to revise one's life plans.

Research has most often considered the consequences of interdependence in the first half of life. For example, research has examined the emotional and financial interdependence between parents and young children. Research has also studied the interdependence of married couples and the relative sacrifices of each member in the realms of family and work. We know much less about the sources and nature of interdependence in later life. The most frequent opinion found in the literature is that relationships in later life are largely enabling, supportive, and essential to well-being. Yet, as noted earlier, we must not forget that the interdependence of lives can also reduce and even foreclose options and that relationships can be burdensome as well as supportive. Nonetheless, we know that loss of close relationships can be devastating to people of any age and that support from other close relationships contributes to the maintenance of a sense that life is meaningful (Rosowsky, 1995). Beyond this, however, we have much to learn about the ways interdependence facilitates meaning in the lives of older people.

As individuals grow older, they change positions in the family structure and with these changes assume new identities, roles, and responsibilities. The nature of relationships with partners, children, and grandchildren may need to be renegotiated over time. The transition to retirement may increase the amount of time that spouses, children, and grandchildren can spend together. Similarly, increased longevity carries the potential for closer family relationships, as family members come to know each other for longer periods of time. Ordinarily these are positive changes, but they may also lead to "long-term lousy relationships" of conflict and even abandonment (Bengtson, Rosenthal, & Burton, 1996, p. 269; Suitor, Pillemer, Keeton, & Robison, 1995; Thomas, 1996b).

The provision of care for the elderly may also create significant challenges for family life. The coupling of increased lifetime with diminished fertility implies that older people may need care for longer periods, but there will be fewer children to provide it. The geographical mobility of children may further attenuate the familial support system available to the elderly. Furthermore, some among the elderly will be childless, most because they never had children, some because they outlived their children (Jerrome, 1996). Where the elderly are in need of care that is not easily available, what may become most meaningful in their lives is simply getting through the day.

We know little as yet about the implications for caregiving of family forms in which the families are based on second marriages or unmarried partnerships. For example, gay and lesbian couples may face special challenges as they age, including making their sexual situations known to health care providers and obtaining insurance in which the partner is the beneficiary (Huyck, 1995; Thomas, 1996a). It may be that today's greater acceptance of gay men and lesbian women will reduce some of these problems. (See, for two case studies, Cohler and Hostetler, this volume.)

Family relationships themselves change as people move into later life. Reduced work and parental responsibilities make possible increases in marital companionship and, often, increases in marital satisfaction (Lee, 1988; Orbuch, House, Mero, & Webster, 1996). Sibling relationships can become more important in later life, especially for women and for men who are single, divorced, widowed, or childless (Connidis, 1994; Wilson, Calsyn, & Orlofsky, 1994). But of special importance to the meaning of later life is the role of grandparent (Thompson, 1993). Grandparenting provides a vehicle for personal growth for both men and women (Thomas, 1994). For many men, grandfatherhood represents an opportunity to express a more nurturing self (Gutmann, 1987) and to compensate for having spent what they, in retrospect, feel was too little time with their own children.

Older people's friendships, like friendships earlier in life, can stem from different settings, take different forms, and fulfill different functions. They are therefore meaningful in very different ways. Older people are likely to have long-term, perhaps lifetime friendships, more recently formed friendships based on work associations or neighboring relationships, and quite short-term friendships based on their current situations. Although some friendships, especially those based on proximity, may be mostly given to exchanges of favors and information, friendships are matters of choice, provide companionship and fun, and, should they become nonsupportive, can be ended (e.g., Field, 1997; Lee & Shehan, 1989). Longstanding friendships in which there are both strong emotional bonds and similarities in values and status tend to provide great satisfaction to older adults (Litwak, 1989; Sperry & Wolfe, 1996). One of the costs imposed by the ill health and frailty that often occurs in the final years of life is a much-restricted friendship network.

Within the family, older women are likely to function as "kinkeepers" (Hagestad, 1986), integrating and fostering family relationships across generations until, upon reaching advanced old age, they turn the role over to daughters (Troll & Bengtson, 1992). Most older women experience widowhood (Uhlenberg, 1980), and women comprise the bulk of the older population. For this reason, and because women may all their lives have maintained relationships with other women, most of the relationships of older women are likely to be with other women.

Older men seem to have more women in their friendship networks than older women have men (Adams, 1994). They are less likely to be widowed than are older women and may be more dependent on their marriages for social integration. They are less likely than women to have become accustomed to confiding in friends (Adams, 1994). If they should become widowed and be without sisters or daughters, they may be at risk of social isolation (Hatch & Bulcroft, 1992).

Residence and Community

There are many benefits to "aging in place" (Fogel, 1993). Remaining at home preserves neighborhood-based social relationships. It facilitates continuing independence and, with it, privacy and control of one's life. There are all the benefits of familiarity. Possessions of sentimental value are retained. The environment that has long sustained one's identity remains present and intact. Yet many elders are required to relocate to new environments because of diminished physical or mental health or dwindling resources. The 1990 census shows that one person in twenty over the age of sixty-five, and fully one person in four over the age of eighty-five, lives in a nursing home. Significant numbers also live in government-subsidized housing or board-and-care homes (Pynoos & Golant, 1996).

Residential change of any kind is difficult for older people. It generally involves separation from family and friends. True, under some circumstances, where people go from a bad situation to better one, residential change can positively affect well-being (Emmons, Colby, & Kaiser, 1998; Kling, Seltzer, & Ryff, 1997). However, it is not uncommon for institutional settings to restrict the type or amount of personal belongings a new resident may bring, to define appropriate styles of dress for residents, and to set rules around visiting, socializing, and even sexual activity. Taking all things together, there is much to be said for providing older people with the resources they need as long as they can reasonably hope to remain in their own homes. These resources may include the support of family members, social services, and help with home modifications and repairs (see Callahan, 1993).

Conclusion

The most pervasive discomfort in later life may not be fear of destitution or even fear of poor health but rather an awareness, perhaps unverbalized, that without obligation life can become empty of meaning; boredom or depression may appear as an accompaniment to loss of purpose or usefulness (Stevens, 1993: Thompson, 1993). Most older adults want to feel that their later years will be as rich in experience and engagement as were their earlier years and that declining health and energy, should they happen, will make for selection among activities rather than disengagement from life. Yet people have to find their own ways to purpose and usefulness: the period of later life is largely without models or pattern. How do people manage?

The framework offered early in this chapter emphasized the need to understand the ways that experiences and meanings are actively created within the confines of biological, psychological, and social constraints. Nevertheless, absent from contemporary scholarship on aging is a conception of the structural sources of experience: the activities and interpretations of activities imposed by schools, workplaces, nursing homes and medical institutions, families and friendship groups, communities, and society at large. This chapter has only begun to explore some of these sources, separating those factors distant from the individual, such as culture, cohort, and demography, from those more proximate, such as family relationships and friendships, leisure and social participation, residence, work and retirement, and education. I have also considered some of the processes within these contexts that set parameters for the experiences and meanings of later life. Finally, I have speculated about the opportunities and barriers to meaningful experiences that exist in these settings.

Following the recent work by the MacArthur Foundation's research network on successful adolescent development (e.g., Jessor, 1993), gerontologists might begin to explore what constitutes a good or bad context for older people, and why and for whom particular contexts matter. We should not assume that everyone would find any given context to be positive or negative or that the worth of a context is easily measured.

However, discussion of the influence of contexts has pushed scholars to more carefully consider the ways that people are shaped by the worlds within which they live.

The comparative freedom from obligation found in later life can foster people's creative exploration of meaningful activity within the limits imposed by their settings, but it can also permit people to continue to live as they always have, though perhaps now at a more leisurely pace and without work or parental responsibilities to structure their time. Or, a third alternative, freedom from obligation can give rise to anomie, boredom, and a sense of pointlessness. We as a society are just now recognizing this issue. The ongoing research described in this chapter, together with the reports of people themselves in later life, may help make for socially and individually meaningful utilization of later life's opportunities.

REFERENCES

Adams, R. G. (1994). Older men's friendship patterns. In E. H. Thompson, Jr. (Ed.), *Older men's lives* (pp. 159–177). Thousand Oaks, CA: Sage.

Bengtson, V., Rosenthal, C., & Burton, L. (1996). Paradoxes of families and aging. In R. Binstock & L. George (Eds.), *Handbook of aging and the social sciences* (4th ed., pp. 253–282). San Diego: Academic Press.

Binstock, R. H., & Day, C. L. (1996). Aging and politics. In R. H. Binstock & L. K. George (Eds.), *Handbook of aging and the social sciences* (4th ed., pp. 362–387). San Diego: Academic Press.

Burkhauser, R., & Quinn, J. (1994). Changing policy signals. In M. W. Riley, R. L. Kahn, & A. Foner (Eds.), *Age and structural lag: Society's failure to provide meaningful opportunities in work, family, and leisure* (pp. 237–262). New York: Wiley.

Callahan, D. (1987). *Setting limits.* New York: Simon & Schuster.

Callahan, J. J., Jr. (1993). Introduction: Aging in place. In J. J. Callahan, Jr. (Ed.), *Aging in place* (pp. 1–4). Amityville, NY: Baywood.

Caro, F., & Bass, S. (1995). Increasing volunteering among older people. In S. Bass (Ed.), *Older and active: How Americans over 55 are contributing to society* (pp. 71–96). New Haven: Yale University Press.

Clausen, J. A. (1995). Gender, contexts, and turning points in adults' lives. In P. Moen, G. H. Elder, Jr., & K. Lüscher (Eds.), *Examining lives in context: Perspectives on the ecology of human development* (pp. 365–389). New York: American Psychological Association.

Connidis, I. A. (1994). Sibling support in older age. *Journal of Gerontology: Social Sciences, 49*(6), S309–317.

Cutler, S., & Hendricks, J. (1990). Leisure and time use across the life course. In R. H. Binstock & L. K. George (Eds.), *Handbook of aging and the social sciences* (3rd ed., pp. 169–185). San Diego: Academic Press.

Eisenhandler, S. A. (1989). More than counting years: Social aspects of time and the identity of elders. In E. L. Thomas (Ed.), *Research on adulthood and aging: The human science approach.* Albany: State University of New York Press.

Elder, G. H., Jr. (1998). The life course and human development. In R. M. Lerner (Ed.), *Handbook of child psychology: Vol. 1. Theoretical models of human development* (5th ed., pp. 939–991). New York: Wiley.

Emmons, R. A., Colby, P. M., & Kaiser, H. A. (1998). When losses lead to gains: personal goals and the recovery of meaning. In P. T. P. Wong & P. S. Fry (Eds.), *The human quest for meaning: A handbook of psychological research and clinical applications* (pp. 163–178). Mahwah, NJ: Erlbaum.

Erikson, E. (1963). *Childhood and society* (2nd ed.). New York: Norton.

Field, D. (1997). Looking back, what period of your life brought you the most satisfaction? *International Journal of Aging and Human Development, 45*(3), 169–194.

Fogel, B. S. (1993). Psychological aspects of staying at home. In J. J. Callahan, Jr. (Ed.), *Aging in place* (pp. 19–28). Amityville, NY: Baywood.

Freund, A., & Smith, J. (1997). Die Selbstdefinition in hohen Alter [Self-definition in old age]. *Zeitschrift für Sozial Psychologie, 28*(1–2), 44–59.

Fry, C. L., Dickerson-Putnam, J., Draper, P., Ikels, C., Keith, J., Glascock, A. P., & Harpending, H. (1997). Culture and the meaning of a good old age. In J. Sokolovsky (Ed.), *The cultural context of aging: Worldwide perspectives* (pp. 99–123). Westport, CT: Bergin & Garvey.

Gradman, T. J. (1994). Masculine identity from work to retirement. In E. H. Thompson, Jr. (Ed.), *Older men's lives* (pp. 104–121). Thousand Oaks, CA: Sage.

Gutmann, D. (1987). *Reclaimed powers: Toward a new psychology of men and women in later life.* New York: Basic Books.

Guy, R. F., & Erdner, R. A. (1993). Retirement: An emerging challenge for women. In R. Kastenbaum (Ed.), *Encyclopedia of adult development* (pp. 405–409). Phoenix, AZ: Oryx Press.

Hagestad, G. O. (1986). The family: Women and grandparents as kin-keepers. In A. Pifer & L. Bronte (Eds.), *Our aging society: Paradox and promise* (pp. 141–160). New York: Norton.

Hagestad, G. O. (1990). Social perspectives on the life course. In R. Binstock & L. George (Eds.), *Handbook of aging and the social sciences* (3rd ed., pp. 151–168). New York: Academic Press.

Hatch, L. R., & Bulcroft, K. (1992). Contact with friends in later life: Disentangling the effects of gender and marital status. *Journal of Marriage and the Family, 54*(1), 222–232.

Heckhausen, J. (1999). *Developmental regulation in adulthood: Age-normative and sociostructural constraints as adaptive challenges.* New York: Cambridge University Press.

Herzog, A. R., Franks, M. M., Markus, H. R., & Holmberg, D. (1998). Activities and well-being in older age: Effects of self-concept and educational attainment. *Psychology and Aging, 13*(2), 179–185.

Hockey, J., & James, A. (1993). *Growing up and growing old: Ageing and dependency in the life course.* Newbury Park, CA: Sage.

Huyck, M. H. (1995). Marriage and close relationships of the marital kind. In R. Bleiszner & V. Bedford (Eds.), *Handbook of aging and the family* (pp. 181–200). Westport, CT: Greenwood Press.

Jerrome, D. (1996). Continuity and change in the study of family relationships. *Ageing and Society, 16*(1), 93–104.

Jessor, R. (1993). Successful adolescent development among youth in high-risk settings. *American Psychologist, 48*(2), 117–126.

Johnson, C. L., & Barer, B. M. (1992). Patterns of engagement and disengagement among the oldest old. *Journal of Aging Studies, 6*(4), 351–364.

Kaufman, S. R. (1993). Values as sources of the ageless self. In R. Kelly (Ed.), *Activity and aging: Staying involved in later life* (pp. 17–24). Newbury Park, CA: Sage.

Keith, J. (1994). Old age and age integration: An anthropological perspective. In M. W. Riley, R. L. Kahn, & A. Foner (Eds.), *Age and structural lag* (pp. 197–216). New York: Wiley.

Keith, J., Fry, C. L., Glascock, A. P., Ikels, C., Dickerson-Putnam, J., Harpending, H. C., & Draper, P. (1994). *The aging experience: Diversity and commonality across cultures.* Newbury Park, CA: Sage.

Kelly, R. (1993). Theory and issues. In R. Kelly (Ed.), *Activity and aging: Staying involved in later life* (pp. 1–4). Newbury Park, CA: Sage.

Kleiber, D. A., & Ray, R. O. (1993). Leisure and generativity. In R. Kelly (Ed.), *Activity and aging: Staying involved in later life* (pp. 106–117). Newbury Park, CA: Sage.

Kling, K. C., Seltzer, M. M., & Ryff, C. D. (1997). Distinctive late-life challenges: Implications for coping and well-being. *Psychology and Aging, 12*(2), 288–295.

Koenig, H. G., Smiley, M., & Gonzales, J. A. P. (1988). *Religion, health, and aging: A review and theoretical integration.* Westport, CT: Greenwood Press.

Kohli, M. (1986). The world we forgot: A historical review of the life course. In V. Marshall (Ed.), *Later life* (pp. 271–303). Beverly Hills, CA: Sage.

Kohli, M. (1994). Work and retirement: A comparative perspective. In M. W. Riley, R. L. Kahn, & A. Foner (Eds.), *Age and structural lag* (pp. 80–106). New York: Wiley.

Lee, G. R. (1988). Marital satisfaction in later life: The effects of nonmarital roles. *Journal of Marriage and the Family, 50*(3), 775–783.

Lee, G. R., & Shehan, C. L. (1989). Social relations and the self-esteem of older persons. *Research on Aging, 11*(4), 427–442.

Little, B. R. (1998). Personal project pursuit: Dimensions and dynamics of personal meaning. In P. T. P. Wong & P. S. Fry (Eds.), *The human quest for meaning: A handbook of psychological research and clinical applications* (pp. 193–212). Mahwah, NJ: Erlbaum.

Litwak, E. (1989). Forms of friendship among older people in an industrial society. In R. G. Adams & R. Blieszner (Eds.), *Older adult friendship: Structure and process* (pp. 65–88). Newbury Park, CA: Sage.

Maddi, S. R. (1998). Creating meaning through decision-making. In P. T. P. Wong & P. S. Fry (Eds.), *The human quest for meaning: A handbook of psychological research and clinical applications* (pp. 1–26). Mahwah, NJ: Erlbaum.

Manheimer, R. J. (1998). The promise and politics of older adult education. *Research on Aging, 20*(4), 391–414.

Manheimer, R. J., Snodgrass, D. D., & Moskow-McKenzie, D. (1995). *Older adult education: A guide to research, programs, and policies*. Westport, CT: Greenwood Press.

McFadden, S. H. (1996). Religion, spirituality, and aging. In J. Birren & K. W. Schaie (Eds.), *Handbook of the psychology of aging* (4th ed., pp. 162–177). San Diego: Academic Press.

McNaught, W., Barth, M. C., & Henderson, P. H. (1991). Older Americans: Willing and able to work. In A. H. Munnell (Ed.), *Retirement and public policy* (pp. 101–114). Dubuque, IA: Kendall/Hunt.

Neugarten, B. L. (1995). The costs of survivorship. *Center on Aging Newsletter*, 11(4), 1. Evanston, IL: Buehler Center on Aging, Northwestern University.

Orbuch, T. L., House, J. S., Mero, R. P., & Webster, P. S. (1996). Martial quality over the life course. *Social Psychology Quarterly*, 59(2), 162–171.

Preston, S. H. (1984). Children and elderly: Divergent paths for America's dependents. *Demography*, 25(6), 44–49.

Pynoos, J., & Golant, S. (1996). Housing and living arrangements for the elderly. In R. H. Binstock & L. K. George (Eds.), *Handbook of aging and the social sciences* (4th ed., pp. 303–324). San Diego: Academic Press.

Quinn, J. F., & Burkhauser, R. V. (1994). Public policy and the plans and preferences of older Americans. *Journal of Aging and Social Policy*, 6(3), 5–20.

Reitzes, D. C., Mutran, E. J., & Fernandez, M. E. (1996). Does retirement hurt well-being? Factors influencing self-esteem and depression among retirees and workers. *Gerontologist*, 36(5), 649–656.

Riley, M. W. (1985). Men, women, and the lengthening of the life course. In A. Rossi (Ed.), *Gender and the life course* (pp. 333–347). New York: Aldine.

Riley, M. W., & Riley, J. (1994). Structural lag: Past and future. In M. W. Riley, R. L. Kahn, & A. Foner (Eds.), *Age and structural lag: Society's failure to provide meaningful opportunities in work, family, and leisure* (pp. 15–36). New York: Wiley.

Rix, S. (1998, May). *Policy challenges*. Presentation at Restructuring Work and the Life Course: An International Symposium, University of Toronto, Toronto, Ontario.

Rosowsky, E. (1995). Sustaining relationships—friends, lovers, and siblings: Will you still need me when I'm old and gray? [Introduction to special issue]. *Journal of Geriatric Psychiatry*, 28(2), 131–137.

Rossi, A. (1986). Sex and gender in an aging society. In A. Pifer & L. Bronte (Eds.), *Our aging society: Paradox and promise* (pp. 111–139). New York: Norton.

Settersten, R. A., Jr. (1997). The salience of age in the life course. *Human Development, 40*(5), 257–281.

Settersten, R. A., Jr. (1999). *Lives in time and place: The problems and promises of developmental science.* Amityville, NY: Baywood.

Settersten, R. A., Jr., & Lovegreen, L. D. (1998). Educational experiences throughout adult life. *Research on Aging, 20(4),* 506–538.

Sørensen, A. (1991). The restructuring of gender relations in an aging society. *Acta Sociologica, 34,* 45–55.

Sperry, L., & Wolfe, P. (1996). The experience of retirement for active older adults. In L. Sperry & H. Prosen (Eds.), *Aging in the twenty-first century: A developmental perspective* (pp. 103–122). New York: Garland.

Stevens, E. S. (1993). Making sense of usefulness: An avenue toward satisfaction in later life. *International Journal of Aging and Human Development, 37*(4), 313–325.

Suitor, J. J., Pillemer, K., Keeton, S., & Robison, J. (1995). Aged parents and aging children: Determinants of relationship quality. In R. Bleiszner & V. Bedford (Eds.), *Handbook of aging and the family* (pp. 223–242). Westport, CT: Greenwood Press.

Szinovacz, M., & Washo, C. (1992). Gender differences in exposure to life events and adaptation to retirement. *Journal of Gerontology: Social Sciences, 47*(4), S191–196.

Thomas, J. L. (1994). Older men as fathers and grandfathers. In E. H. Thompson, Jr. (Ed.), *Older men's lives* (pp. 197–217). Thousand Oaks, CA: Sage.

Thomas, J. L. (1996a). Expanding knowledge of older gay men and lesbians. In L. Sperry & H. Prosen (Eds.), *Aging in the twenty-first century: A developmental perspective* (pp. 141–152). New York: Garland.

Thomas, J. L. (1996b). Relationships with children, grandchildren, and great-grandchildren: Today and tomorrow. In L. Sperry & H. Prosen (Eds.), *Aging in the twenty-first century: A developmental perspective* (pp. 153–164). New York: Garland.

Thompson, P. (1993). "I don't feel old": The significance of the search for meaning in later life. *International Journal of Geriatric Psychiatry, 8*(8), 685–692.

Torres-Gil, F. M. (1992). *The new aging: Politics and change in America.* Westport, CT: Auburn House.

Tornstam, L. (1997). Gerotranscendence: The contemplative dimension of aging. *Journal of Aging Studies, 11*(2), 143–154.

Troll, L. E., & Bengtson, V. L. (1992). The oldest-old in families: An intergenerational perspective. *Generations, 16*(3), 39–44.

Uhlenberg, P. (1980). Death and the family. *Journal of Family History, 5,* 313–320.

Wallace, S. P., Williamson, J. B., Lung, R. G., & Powell, L. A. (1991). A lamb in wolf's clothing? The reality of senior power and social policy. In M. Minkler & C. L. Estes (Eds.), *Critical perspectives on aging: The political and moral economy of growing old* (pp. 95–114). Amityville, NY: Baywood.

Wilson, J. G., Calsyn, R. J., & Orlofsky, J. L. (1994). Impact of sibling relationships on social support and morale of the elderly. *Journal of Gerontological Social Work, 22*(3–4), 157–170.

Wong, P. T. P. (1998). Spirituality, meaning, and successful aging. In P. T. P. Wong & P. S. Fry (Eds.), *The human quest for meaning: A handbook of psychological research and clinical applications* (pp. 359–394). Mahwah, NJ: Erlbaum.

Wong, P. T. P., & Fry, P. S. (Eds.) (1998). *The human quest for meaning: A handbook of psychological research and clinical applications.* Mahwah, NJ: Erlbaum.

FIVE

Aging, Place, and Meaning in the Face of Changing Circumstances

Graham D. Rowles and Hege Ravdal

EDITORS' INTRODUCTION Rowles and Ravdal provide us with a detailed description of our bonds to place and possessions. Should we move from one home to another, as happens often in the Third Age, we may discover that loss of familiar places and objects unsettles us. In the middle of the night we may wake uncertain of our location: uncertain whether we are still where we once lived or have instead been transported to a place that is new and momentarily baffling.

Past places continue to exist in memory, sometimes more strongly than places in our current lives. One of the editors can remember vividly sensations from his boyhood home: the cold metal of the latch to the storm door in back, the thick carpet on the stairway downstairs, the emphatic sound of the garage door's closing. These memories are part of him. In the same way, the older person who moves to be nearer the children, or to a home that is easier to care for, will continue to be aware of the home that was left.

At one level we all recognize the importance of belongings: photographs and other possessions. We spend a lifetime acquiring them. Often, these objects remind us of the experiences that constituted our past and of accomplishments we still take pride in. They help situate the present as a continuation of the past. Loss of such objects constitutes loss of anchors to identity.

Anyone who has moved knows how hard it is to become reestablished in a new community: to settle into a new place, make new friends, establish new patterns of shopping and leisure. We expect ourselves to be resilient, and normally we are. But moving from one place to another is ordinarily not without cost in uncertainty, occasional frustration, and—if the move takes us far from our previous home—occasional loneliness.

Insofar as it is possible, most people want to age in place, and they seem to do better if they can. Rowles and Ravdal call the effort to provide special housing for the aged "myopic beneficence." It may happen, as someone moves into the Fourth Age, that some sort of assisted living becomes necessary. But until that happens, most prefer to remain in what they know in their bones is their home.

Meaning in our lives is intimately bound up with personal history. Our personal history, in turn, is inextricably bound up with the places of our lives. A visit to the haunts of childhood evokes nostalgia—re-creation in our minds of the ambiance of the yard where we played, the tree (now chopped down) where we carved our initials, and the bench by the post office where we waited for the school bus (Chawla, 1992; Hart, 1979). Attending the graduation of a niece at our alma mater reintroduces us to the setting where we struggled with calculus during the college days that forged our identity. Passing the gravesite of a fallen comrade who did not survive the Vietnam conflict reminds us of our own good fortune. Returning "home" to our dwelling after an extended absence evokes feelings of warmth and infuses us with a sense of belonging, reflecting the plethora of personal meanings with which our abode has become imbued.

Most of the time we do not consciously acknowledge the role of places as repositories of meaning in our lives. Rather, the essence of the meaning of place is implicit and taken for granted. Indeed, for many people, the meaning of place only becomes truly apparent through the reflective lens of time. Like interpersonal relationships, the meaning of place is often highlighted and accentuated through separation (Brown & Perkins, 1992; Fried, 1963). The death or departure of a friend may leave a void, a sense of emptiness and loss. As, through reminiscence, we process and appraise our recollections of the relationship, its meaning evolves as a component of our life. We create and re-create the meaning of the relationship in a manner consonant with our sense of self and the "place" of the friend in our life. This re-creation is part of the ongoing re-definition of who we are (Kaufman, 1986). And so, too, with the places of our life: meaning generally only becomes fully apparent during times of separation and with the vision of hindsight. As we forge an ongoing autobiography through selective memory and reinterpretation of life events, we reintegrate those places where meaningful events transpired and became part of the mosaic of our identity.

In this chapter, we explore the meaning of place in old age as it evolves in response to changing personal and environmental circumstances. Specifically, we focus on the way change in geographical location, both forced and voluntary, may result in a transition in the very meaning of elders' lives as they accommodate, sometimes more successfully than at other times, to changing personal circumstances associated with their aging.

In this context, change in geographical location may be of two types (Scheidt & Norris-Baker, 1999). It may be indigenous: change may result from deterioration of the dwelling or disruption and transformation of the character and ambiance of a neighborhood as an interstate highway is routed through its core or as an unfamiliar ethnic group filters into the area. In other words, the geographical location may change while the individual remains in place. Change in geographical location may also result from relocation to a new setting through either a local move or long-distance migration (Wiseman & Roseman, 1979).

In an increasingly transitional and mobile society, both types of environmental change are ever more common; indeed, they are normative expectations in the life course of most people. Most elders are able to harness the wisdom of environmental experience in creating and recreating meaning in place as they pass through the different settings of their lives. However, some elders are more successful than others in undertaking this process of "place-making" (McHugh & Mings, 1996). For some, adaptation to changing residential circumstances—for example, a move to a nursing facility—simply continues a lifelong process of successively adapting to new places. It represents little more than an opportunity for opening up new "horizons of meaning" in the rich tapestry of their life (Gubrium, 1993). For others, particularly those who through their life course have had limited experience with relocation or who over a lifetime of residential inertia have developed strong attachment to a single location, change in geographical location (either indigenous or as a result of relocation) can be traumatic. In these cases, it may be important to intervene so that elders can retain vestigial elements of the meaning of former environments. At the same time, such interventions should facilitate the creation and nurturing of new meanings of place that foster environmental affinity within the new setting.

The Meaning of Place

What exactly do we mean when we talk about the meaning of place and how is such meaning integrated within the larger context of elders' lives? During the past two decades research has begun to provide some answers (see, e.g., Boschetti, 1985, 1990, 1995; Cuba, 1989; Cuba & Hummon, 1993; Howell, 1983; Norris-Baker & Scheidt, 1991, 1994; Rowles, 1978, 1983a, 1983b, 1990, 1991, 1993; Rubinstein, 1987, 1989, 1990; Scheidt, 1993; Scheidt & Norris-Baker, 1990, 1993, 1999; Seamon, 1979, 1980; Wheeler, 1995). Several distinctive themes have emerged from this literature.

First, there is the notion that individuals develop a sense of physical intimacy and comfort in settings they routinely traverse on a daily basis over an extended period (O'Bryant, 1982, 1983; Rowles, 1983b). Passing over the same paths both within and beyond the dwelling day after day leads to a level of physiological familiarity that may transcend consciousness, something David Seamon (1979, 1980) termed "body subject." As I type this manuscript, I do not consciously select each key. Rather, familiarity with the process allows me to relegate the selection of each letter to my subconscious. Driving down the freeway becomes an "automatic" process. I may suddenly become aware that I have successfully negotiated many miles while daydreaming. Such familiarity is adaptive for elders in that it may allow them to continue to move through spaces that might otherwise be beyond their cognitive capability to negotiate. As one of Shirley L. O'Bryant's subjects noted, "I can walk around my place in the dark because I know where everything is" (O'Bryant, 1982, p. 352). Indeed, there is a growing literature on the theme of the adaptive benefits of routine and habitual behavior (Kielhofner, 1995; Ludwig, 1997).

A second component of the meaning of place involves social immersion, the transformation of physical spaces into social places. Places assume meaning on this level in a number of overlapping ways. A place may become a behavior setting in which the environment conditions a characteristic pattern of use and social interaction that is culturally prescribed and that repeats itself regardless of the particular actors involved (Barker, 1968; Barker & Barker, 1961; Norris-Baker, 1998, 1999; Seamon & Nordin, 1980). Distinctive forms of social interaction may come to characterize particular environments. Interactions with a friend during a chance meeting at the mall differ from the way we might interact with the same person in the hushed sanctuary of our church or the deafening ambiance of a contemporary nightclub. Places also come to assume social meaning over time as a result of shared residence. Over the years, the content and tone of frequent interactions with neighbors imbue the neighborhoods where we reside with a social ambiance, a personality borne of cultural and social norms and expectations. The reserved social distancing of an upper-class residential enclave fosters an entirely different ambiance from the bustling street activity and cosmopolitan atmosphere of some inner-city neighborhoods. Embedded within each neighborhood are social relationships among neighbors and those who live within their vicinity (Halperin, 1998; Keller, 1969; Suttles, 1968). Relationships on this level may be frequent and intense. They may involve systems of mutual reciprocity and caring that convey a sense of social belonging arising from years of face-to-face interactions and social exchanges (Jacobs, 1961; Rowles, 1981). On this level, local place may come to hold great social meaning for its residents (Hummon, 1990). As Lee Cuba and David Hummon elaborate in their discussion of social aspects of place identity, "Place identities affiliate the self with significant roles, bringing a sense of belonging and order to one's sociospatial world" (1993, p. 113).

While the meaning and personality of locales are often defined on a social level, place meaning is ultimately an extremely personal phenomenon. It is intimately bound up with autobiography. Particularly for elders who are longtime residents of a particular setting, places have a time-depth reflecting the accumulation of memories of myriad events that transpired in the setting. Over decades of residence, a sense of autobiographical insideness, of being part of the places of one's life and of the places being a part of the self, becomes taken for granted (Rowles, 1980, 1983b). This conveys a sense of identity and helps provide a sense of permanence in a world that may be changing, both as a physical setting and, with the death of age peers, as a social context in the present. In a sense, the environment(s) one inhabits remain as a testament to one's life. The selective and repeated mental reconstruction and maintenance of these places in consciousness, a habit of the mind, provides a sense of reinforcement of the self.

Developing meaning through place is not a passive process. Most individuals play an active role in creating the places of their lives. This is particularly the case with respect to places that are possessed or controlled, such as a person's room or residence. Here, there is discretion to create personal place, to transform a "house" into a "home" by imbuing it with meaning. Through the very process of "dwelling" in a residence it is transformed from a space, a simple physical structure, to a place suffused with the warmth of relationships and experience (Young, 1998). From being a mere shelter, it becomes a key element in the relationship between an individual and his or her environment. As Kimberly Dovey (1985, p. 43) puts it, "Home is a schema of relationships that brings order, integrity and meaning to experience in place—a series of connections between person and world."

For many, home becomes a sacred place (Altman & Werner, 1985; Bachelard, 1994; Buttimer, 1980; Eliade, 1959; Young, 1998). Home acquires special meaning not only as a result of special events that transpired within its walls but also as a living museum of the occupants' lives where treasured artifacts and identity-defining personal possessions are stored and displayed (Belk, 1992; Boschetti, 1995; Paton & Cram, 1992; Rubinstein, 1989). By surrounding themselves with such physical cues to the events of their lives, elders, like others, make places meaningful. The proudly displayed photographs of grandchildren, the Navajo sand painting purchased on a fondly remembered Arizona vacation, the New England Hitchcock wooden chairs received as a wedding gift, by transforming the space of the home into a gallery of the occupants' lives, contribute to imbuing the space with personal significance. Viewing each artifact or memento can resurrect in the occupants' consciousness the events and, by extension, the places, of their lives. This process can transform space that to an outsider might seem mundane into a vibrant repository of meaning.

Longtime residence can also create a sense of autobiographical affinity with the space beyond the home. For elders, the surveillance zone—space that can be viewed from the window—may come to assume special meaning (Jacobs, 1961; Rowles, 1981). Within this zone, neighbors within each other's visual field may monitor each other's behavior and develop special relationships involving the mutual exchange of care and concern in times of need. Although characteristically less intense, comparable levels of personal meaning and affinity may be attributed to the neighborhood beyond (Gans, 1962; Gittel & Vidal, 1998; Suttles, 1968).

Physical intimacy, social immersion, and autobiographical memory contribute to what Malcolm P. Cutchin has termed "experiential place integration" (Cutchin, 1997a, p. 1661; see also Cutchin, 1997b; Howell, 1983; Rowles, 1991). This is a blending of place and self within an overall sense of being in place (Rowles, 1991). For some people, particularly those who have resided in a single location throughout their lives, being in place fosters a strong sense of possessiveness, even territoriality. Such intense bonding with places leads to a reluctance to abandon them because, in an almost literal sense, to abandon them is to abandon the self. Others, frequently those who have led more itinerant lives, may experience far less intense bonding with place. Indeed, it has been suggested that contemporary mobile society can generate a sense of placelessness—of being out of place (Relph, 1976).

Each individual's level of being in place is both dynamic and adaptive. It involves a continuous reweaving and refinement of patterns of use of space, environmental images, emotional attachments, and vicarious involvement in locations displaced in space and time (Rowles, 1978). Within this experiential rubric, the meaning of place evolves as individual circumstances change. Sandra Howell provides a good example of this process as manifest in the short term.

> A person may, for example, see in a shop window a vintage
> table lamp and laughingly say to a companion, "We had a
> lamp like that when I was a kid," which, in turn, initiates a
> flood of place—event—people memories, some of which
> are allowed to emerge as verbal reminiscence, some as fleet-
> ing imagery, but all contextually selective. The affective
> meaning may begin as positive associations and weave, in
> and out, through a range of emotions. (1983, p. 100)

More stable manifestations of being in place evolve over a longer term. Over an extended period, characteristically measured in months and years rather than moments, patterns of physical intimacy, social immersion, and autobiographical insideness evolve through repetition into an array of resilient routine behaviors and established meanings of place. It has been suggested that such resiliency is adaptive in old age because it provides a level of contextual comfort that allows elders to accommodate more easily to their changing physical, psychological, and social capabilities (Rowles, 1983b; Rubinstein & Parmalee, 1992). Indeed, this aspect of being in place has provided the underlying rationale for current policies in the United States that view aging in place as an optimal residential model for growing old (Rowles, 1993).

Aging in Place

The idea of aging in place may ultimately be viewed as reflective of a basic human need for territoriality (Ardrey, 1966). However, the more recent emergence of aging in place as an underpinning of public sentiment and policy is closely linked to societal recognition of the role of ownership and attachment to place, and to the presumed need for the familiar, as adaptive features of aging. Grounded in the residential inertia of an agrarian nineteenth-century American population (more Americans lived in rural than urban settings until 1920), the notion of aging in place most likely had its origins in strong ties to the land emanating from homesteading and taking possession of the frontier. During the Great Depression and in the immediate post–World War II era, the idea of ownership and attachment to place was reinforced by the growth of suburbia and the emergence of the American dream of home ownership. In the two decades between 1940 and 1960, owner-occupied units as a percentage of all occupied units increased from 43% to 62% (Callahan, 1992, p. 5). By 1988, 75% of the 19.5 million households headed by elders were owner-occupied (AARP/AoA, 1989).

Somewhat surprisingly, these trends, which would seem entirely consonant with an ethos of aging in place, do not seem, at least initially, to have been paralleled by public approval of aging in place as the optimum circumstance for growing old. Indeed, Rowles (1993) has argued that the emergence of special housing options for elders during the 1960s and 1970s, the visibility of debates on the desirability of age-segregated versus age-integrated housing for elders, and the phenomenal growth of the nursing home industry (given impetus by the passage of the Older Americans Act in 1965) reflected precisely the opposite. During the post–World War II era, instead of approval for aging in place, there developed a paternalistic perspective that elders needed to be "cared for": provided with special supportive housing options and, as they became more frail, relocated to successively more supportive (often medically oriented) environments. There was an implicit assumption that elders were willing to relocate—or at least accepted the wisdom of relocating—as they became increasingly frail. These trends generated an erroneous public image that relocation was a normative and expected attendant of growing old. Notions of the meaningfulness of lifelong residence amid friends in a familiar setting seem to have been overridden by a charitable but myopic beneficence.

In reality, the majority of elders do not and never have relocated, and fewer than half spend any time in a nursing facility (Kemper & Murtaugh, 1991). Yet, only in the most recent two decades has the realization that most elders prefer to age in place been translated into policy. Over the past fifteen years a proliferation of both research literature and public policy initiatives has reinforced the idea of aging in place as a focus of aging policy (Callahan, 1992; Fogel 1992; Rowles, 1993; Tilson, 1990). By 1990 Jon Pynoos (1990) was able to identify more than ninety federal programs that he considered reflected an underlying belief in the desirability of aging in place.

It is important to acknowledge that aging in place is not a static phenomenon. It is not merely an expression of inertia, of a desire to remain in a familiar home. Rather, aging in place is a dynamic phenomenon best understood as an outcome of ongoing interaction among a complex set of interdependent factors. While aging in place may frequently have been viewed as a form of locational status quo, it is in fact a dynamic relationship between a person and his or her environment. As M. Powell Lawton (1990) noted, aging in place is "a transaction between an aging individual and his or her residential environment that is characterized by changes in both person and environment over time, with the physical location of the person being the only constant" (p. 288). According to Lawton, aging in place requires repeated reaffirmation and redefinition of locational affiliation throughout this process in response to physical, psychological, social, and environmental changes. Not only is the individual experiencing intrinsic changes, but he or she must also simultaneously relate to extrinsic changes in the structure of the residence, in the surrounding natural and physical environment, and in the people who surround him or her.

Extending this temporal theme, the process of aging in place must be understood in relationship to the span of the individual's life course. Key places in one's life serve as cues to identity and reminders of the key features of one's biography (Rubinstein & Parmalee, 1992). These places provide a spatial structure, a geographical context, around which life experience can be organized. Over time, emotional ties to place grow in strength as individual locations accumulate layer upon layer of meanings from the events that transpired within them. As a result, it is logical to assume that with increasing age and length of residence in a single location, attachment to place tends to intensify and the desire to age in place tends to be reinforced (McHugh & Mings, 1996).

In spite of the many accommodations and adjustments that elders and their families make in order to remain in a familiar setting, there comes a point when, for many elders, aging in place is no longer a viable option. Changing personal circumstances—including failing physical abilities, declining health, the death of a spouse, relocation of children, a thinning local network of age peers, or loss of income following retirement—can jeopardize an elder's ability to remain in place. The impact of such personal changes may be exacerbated by environmental changes: the dwelling may deteriorate, supportive neighbors depart, and the neighborhood decline.

Environmental Change

Environmental changes are often beyond the control of the individual. Familiar and socially supportive neighborhoods change as the basis of their economy is eroded or as new ethnic or cultural groups move in to occupy the space. For example, in the rural Appalachian community where Rowles conducted an extended field study (1983a, 1983b), elders were aging in place in a very different community from the one where they had spent their childhood. Lifelong residents could remember the time before the Great Depression when Colton had been a thriving and bustling railroad and coal mining community of more than eight hundred residents. The prized photographs of this community of their past, proudly displayed on the mantle, revealed a place that contrasted with the quiet, run-down rural "bedroom" community of slightly over four hundred persons where they now (1980) resided, with its abandoned homes and boarded stores. As Colton's elders aged in place, change in the theater of their lives had occurred gradually over several decades. Most of the elders had been able to adjust and to preserve the meaning of the place as a backdrop to their lives. They had been able to retain, to embellish, and to intensify the meanings with which their homes and community were imbued.

In some cases, change is far more rapid and disruptive of individuals' ability to successfully age in place. The devastation of large-scale urban renewal, routing of a new highway through a neighborhood, or a natural disaster can destroy a home or a neighborhood and with it the physical cues and markers of attachment that made it a repository of meaning (Brown & Perkins, 1992; Detzner, Bell, & Stum, 1991; Fried, 1963).

Elders accommodate to personal and environmental change in a variety of ways. For some, the meaning of place is maintained through a process of "holding on" as the individual makes lifestyle adjustments in order to remain in familiar surroundings (Rowles, 1983a). This may become manifest through strategies of personal accommodation. Such strategies include closing off upstairs rooms to avoid the need to climb too taxing stairs. They also include arranging for a neighbor to do grocery shopping, pick up a prescription from the pharmacy, or bring in the mail from the roadside mailbox. Elders may vigorously resist community change by banding together with their neighbors to oppose the routing of a highway through their neighborhood or oppose a zoning change that threatens their homes.

In some cases, elders who remain in place may accommodate to changing environmental circumstances by creating new roles and meanings that facilitate continued aging in place within a transformed environment. In studies of declining small rural Kansas towns, Carolyn Norris-Baker and Rick J. Scheidt (Norris-Baker, 1999; Norris-Baker & Scheidt, 1991; Scheidt & Norris-Baker, 1990, 1993) have illustrated how those elders who have aged in place have created a new elder-centered behavior setting with a distinctive lifestyle and culture. With the departure of significant segments of the younger population, they have assumed new leadership roles within the community—taking over civic and community projects and keeping open cafes and stores that would otherwise have closed. "A heightened sense of environmental mastery and self-efficacy provides benefits as well as risks for some older individuals. Population decline offers opportunities for older residents who desire to fill resulting role vacancies" (Scheidt & Norris-Baker, 1993, p. 341). In the process, the elders of these small towns have created new social and personal meaning in the place they are determined to make the final locale of their lives.

Finally, elders may be able to retain the meaning of the places of their lives in the face of radical transformations in these environments by continuing to vicariously inhabit them as they were in the past (Rowles, 1978). The lifelong elder residents of Winchester Street, a run-down inner-city neighborhood in New England, were able to sustain a strong sense of attachment and belonging to their neighborhood because they were able to retain a shared sense of the community as it had been. This did not involve denial of the dangerous and deteriorated character of the contemporary physical setting. Rather, it entailed maintaining the aura and meaning of the neighborhood of the past through both telephone and face-to-face communication among elders who had shared in the supportive and community-oriented social ambiance of this place during the 1930s and 1940s. For these elders, the neighborhood of the past still existed; it continued to live in their consciousness and conversations and to have great meaning as the stage on which key elements of their lives had been played out.

Relocation

A second response to changing personal circumstances is to relocate. Although most elders are reluctant to move, changes in the post–World War II economy that led to increases in discretionary income in retirement produced a significant group of elders who could afford to migrate to high-amenity areas (Longino, 1995). As a result, locales throughout the United States, including Cape Cod, the hills of western North Carolina, the Ozark Mountains region of Arkansas, lakeshore areas in northern Michigan, and the Lake Havasu area of Arizona, have emerged as popular destinations for affluent retirees (Cuba, 1989; Haas, 1990; Rowles & Watkins, 1993). Increased affluence and mobility have also facilitated voluntary return migration as elders go "home" to childhood locations in order to retire (Serow & Charity, 1988; White, 1987). Finally, with increased life expectancy, growing numbers of elders are now living with levels of disability that force them to make involuntary short-distance moves into assisted living or long-term care environments. For these elders, relocation is an attendant process to their aging. By the end of the 1980s more than 1.9 million elderly householders, representing 9.6% of the nation's householders aged 65 and older, were living in low-rent federally subsidized housing (Golant, 1992). In addition, by 1985 there were 19,000 nursing home facilities in the United States with 1.6 million beds (Strahan, 1987).

In the context of our focus on meaning, it is useful to summarize studies of late-life relocation within the rubric of a life-course model of aging (McHugh & Mings, 1996; Rubinstein & Parmelee, 1992). This perspective posits that different types of moves are associated with changing circumstances within the life course. Expectations regarding residential pathways emerge early in life. There develops an expectation that we will leave home to attend college, that we will relocate as we marry and establish a family, that we will contemplate purchasing a place to retire as our children leave home, and that we may need to move to a more supportive environment as frailty increases. Indeed, relocations throughout the life course and especially in later life are manifestations of a lifetime of expectations and experiences arrayed along a broadly anticipated normative trajectory. While we may form attachments with new places at any time, bonds already formed continue to play a part in the evolving relationship of life course and place. As Robert L. Rubinstein and Patricia A. Parmelee express it, "place attachment is not a state but a process that continues throughout life." In elaborating on this theme, they write:

Intersecting here, then, are diverse elements that include the socially constructed life course (culturally defined standards for what constitutes a life course and its key events); the personally experienced life course (how one uniquely traverses and interprets the life course); and the perceived relation of the life course to place. The latter relation is central to place attachment but it is highly fluid in that the nature and strength of bonds with the environment change with the individual's evolving experiences and developmental tasks. (1992, p. 143)

Many studies link relocation to distinct life-course events as a means of organizing the patterns that emerge when looking at migration and mobility across age groups. Although some researchers have resisted the desire to group elders in terms of residential mobility, claiming that doing so obscures the continuum of the life course (Clark & Davies, 1990), many see such conceptualization as a means to understand a complex and multifaceted phenomenon. According to the typology of elderly migration of Eugene Litwak and Charles F. Longino (1987), older people make three basic types of moves, each characterized by key life events and triggering mechanisms. The first type, *amenity migration*, tends to follow retirement fairly closely and is motivated for the most part by considerations of lifestyle and continuing good health. A second move typically occurs when the elder develops moderate forms of disability and performance of daily tasks becomes difficult. The need to move may be exacerbated by the loss of a spouse and is often motivated by deteriorating health and by the desire to be near family members who can provide practical as well as social support. This type of move, which may be characterized as an *independence maintenance move,* is closely linked to notions of functional health but not yet to the need for institutional care. The third type of move, often a final relocation, is triggered by increasing severity of chronic disabilities and a corresponding limitation in the ability of kin resources to maintain the individual in a community setting. The situation necessitates a *dependency move* to an institutional setting, often initiated for the now dependent elder by family members. In contrast with amenity and maintenance related migration, such moves are typically local. They are often involuntary.

Not all elders make all three types of relocation. The majority of elders never move for reasons of amenity, although those who do have received considerable attention in the migration literature (Cuba & Longino, 1991; McHugh & Mings, 1996; Rowles & Watkins, 1993). However, many elders do make at least one of the moves in response to changing circumstances. What is important in this context is that all three types of move share the characteristic of severance from familiar place.

Recent trends in migration behavior have added a new level of complexity in exploring the relationship between elders, place, and the life course. In an increasingly mobile society, growing numbers of elders are residing in multiple locations. Particularly for a cadre of seasonal migrants, both "snowbirds" and "sunbirds," annual residence is split between two or more locations. For these elders, aging in place and migration are no longer mutually exclusive. Kevin E. McHugh and Robert C. Mings (1996, p. 530) have documented how "[e]lders may reside in multiple locales, forging place attachments and experiences via seasonal migration and recurring mobility." They maintain that the simple dichotomy between aging in place and migration fails to capture the multilocational nature of place attachments and meanings of "home" among a growing number of seasonally migratory elders. The meaning of place, in the context of residence in multiple locations, is also discussed by Cuba and Hummon in their study of elderly migrants to Cape Cod (Cuba & Hummon, 1993). They note that definition of alternative locales often involves differences in environmental scale (home, neighborhood, community, and region) and the superimposition of multiple settings that to a greater or lesser extent are viewed as "home."

Transporting Meaning

What are the processes whereby elders maintain meaning through the places of their lives as they accommodate to changing circumstances over their life course and to their aging? The answer to this question, acknowledging the dynamism of the life course, is that, in addition to creating new meanings in each environment they experience, elders carry the legacies and baggage of their former affiliations with previous settings where they have resided. They transport meaning with them and draw on prior experience in accommodating to each new environment (McHugh & Mings, 1996; Shumaker & Conti, 1985; Wheeler, 1996; Young, 1998).

In an innovative in-depth study of eight elders who moved to a North Carolina continuing-care retirement community, W. Michael Wheeler (1995) provides clear documentation of these processes. He found that, without exception, his informants' feelings toward their new residence, the essence of their being in place, contained "a significant number of the positive influencing factors that they identified with past residential places" (p. 116). Distinctive themes pertaining to both the physical and social environments inhabited over the course of their residential histories were found to permeate the process of transference and place-making. In summarizing the cumulative transfer of place meanings over the life course, Wheeler concludes:

> A relationship exists between an individual's feelings about past residential experiences and his/her feelings about his current place of residence. With the exception of health-

related concerns, which for most informants became more important as they neared retirement, factors related to the physical and social environments experienced in the informants' first place of residence can be identified in their current place of residence. Each subsequent residential experience is added to the individual's information base. The information, in turn, is used as a reference by the individual throughout his or her entire life. (p. 119)

What are the mechanisms of this transference? Perhaps the most important is memory—both conscious memory and the implicit "body subject" recall of our lifelong environmental experience (Seamon, 1980). We selectively remember the places of our life in the process of constructing our contemporary self. While we may never again experience the thrill of graduation, we can envision the aura of the assembly hall as we accepted the diploma. Though the house of our childhood may have been razed to the ground, we can still visualize the nooks and crannies of the attic where we played. We can almost smell the aroma of the freshly baked bread in the kitchen. Such constructed memories are carried with us into each new setting. Each new setting becomes suffused with this aura of the past as we create and recreate meaning in the places of our contemporary lives.

Beyond conscious memory, the implicit meaning embedded in the physical comfort of a familiar setting, our sense of "body subject" (Seamon, 1980), may be adaptively transferred with us when we relocate to a new setting. In the short term, when we stay at an unfamiliar motel with our spouse we may, without thinking, naturally choose the same side of the bed on which we sleep when at home. Upon moving into a new apartment we may arrange our furniture in a manner remarkably similar to its relative placement in our former residence (Hartwigsen, 1987). Such implicit place memory is an often subconscious accommodation to changing circumstance.

Placed in life-course perspective, the process of meaningful place-making as an amalgam of the places of our past is facilitated by a variety of practical mechanisms that provide reinforcement to the maintenance of identity. One of the most important is the transference of possessions and artifacts that enhance our comfort level and trigger the resurrection in consciousness of the places of our past. There is a growing literature on the role of possessions as key facilitators of place creation (Belk, 1992; Boschetti, 1995; Csikszentmihalyi & Rochberg-Halton, 1981; Paton & Cram, 1992; Young, 1998). The importance of familiar artifacts extends far beyond the value of taking our own pillow to an unfamiliar motel to ease our entrance into sleep. In her classic study of Victoria Plaza in San Antonio, Texas, Frances Carp (1966) poignantly recorded the dilemma of an elderly couple relocating from their house into an apartment, as they struggled with the selection of appropriate items to take to the new residence.

> A few applicants showed they would experience a painful wrench at letting go of furniture and other possessions which had, for so long, been part of their lives. One couple at last faced, during the tour, what they had tried not to think about, for as long as possible—the obvious fact that the apartment could not accommodate their huge and ornate furniture and the collection of dishes, silver, pictures, and curios which dated from their courtship and recorded their fifty-odd years of marriage.
>
> Stiff and white-faced at the end of the tour, they confided to their interviewer that, had they been able to locate any place they could afford, in which they could live with their "own things," they would have chosen it without hesitation and let someone else have the beautiful new apartment. However, they had exhausted all possibilities and had no option. Heartbroken, they would part with their beautiful beloved things and buy small, inexpensive, strange pieces. (pp. 89–90)

The role of possessions as elements of identity, the potential of such possessions to infuse places with meaning, and the stresses and opportunities involved in giving up treasured possessions are further reinforced by studies that have begun to explore the phenomenon of divestiture and its phenomenological meaning to elders (Morris, 1992).

Creating Meaning in Place: Opportunities for Intervention?

Some elders accommodate to personal and environmental change with great success. They are able to adapt to new settings and to find meaning in every new environment they inhabit. Others, particularly those who relocate or are relocated against their will, experience significant stress, even trauma, in moving to a new environment. As documented in a substantial and somewhat controversial literature on relocation stress, environmental change often leads to measurable increases in morbidity and mortality among those who had been reluctant to move (Aldrich & Mendkoff, 1963; Danermark & Ekstrom, 1990; Horowitz & Schulz, 1983). It is our contention that one important contributing component to such negative outcomes of relocation is the inability of these elders to transport or to create new meaning in the settings to which they move. This inability can be addressed through more sensitive recognition of the role of the meaning of place in sustaining well-being. What can be done to facilitate the transportation of extant meanings or the creation or recreation of meaning in new settings? In this section we provide a summary of strategies to minimize the likelihood that separation from familiar place will become a pathological separation from self.

Some possible interventions are very concrete. In designing living spaces for elders we have learned to create spaces that accommodate physical disabilities and provide physical supports for the frail. However, contemporary design seems to have ignored issues of sustaining meaning in elders' lives. In both community and institutional settings, we should seek to design spaces that can become places, by making ample provision for the storage and display of treasured photographs and artifacts that link elders to their pasts and provide a source of ongoing meaning in their lives (Hunt & Pastalan, 1987). A few extra shelves and the provision of opportunities to personalize space may significantly enhance well-being.

Too often, elders are relocated without adequate warning or preparation. While in some situations this may be inevitable (the result of a sudden health crisis or an environmental disaster), in many cases there is ample opportunity to provide supportive counseling and, through "place therapy" (Scheidt & Norris-Baker, 1999), to work with the elder to minimize the stress of a move. A variety of relocation preparation programs have been proposed and implemented; they include anticipatory environmental simulations, preliminary visits to the new setting, and provision of supportive counseling (Dickinson, 1996; Hunt & Pastalan, 1987; Lawton, 1998; Pastalan, Davis, & Haberkorn, 1975). Unfortunately, such programs do not always focus on the meaning of the move and the role of individual personality and temperament in determining successful environmental adjustment. They tend, perhaps through ignorance, to underestimate the role that the transference or nurturing of place-making may play in increasing the likelihood of a successful move.

Attempts to understand the underlying dimensions of the meaning an individual attaches to the environment from which that person is relocating, linked to a genuine effort to facilitate the transference of as many elements of such place affinity as possible, may significantly enhance the person's post-move adjustment. Barbara B. Brown and Douglas D. Perkins (1992) have written:

> Although research on the preparation for relocation is sparse, it suggests that advance efforts to start relinquishing old ties and anticipating or developing new ties and identities will help reduce the disruption. Furthermore, these efforts involve cognitive, affective and behavioral processes that serve to reaffirm some and relinquish other aspects of former attachments. (p. 288)

We can point to several very pragmatic strategies for accomplishing the transfer and recreation of elements of place meaning. There is now ample evidence that the selective transfer of treasured possessions that provide ongoing cues to an elder's identity, especially photographs, can significantly ease the transition and enhance postrelocation well-being (McCracken, 1987; Wapner, Demick & Redondo, 1990). In her discussion of the recreation of place attachment and meaning following relocation by a sample of Swedish elders, Clare Cooper Marcus (1992) explains:

> If people were able to re-create the interior of their old home in the new apartment, and to find a parallel in the layout of rooms—and therefore in their daily routine—they were also more likely to adjust positively to the move. For example, Mr. Knutson had a great love of nature and animals, and was happy when his new apartment very much resembled his old home with floral patterns on sofa and bedspread, large tropical houseplants, views of landscapes, and photos of endangered animals. Similarly, Mrs. Lihnas, at 88, made a very positive adjustment to her new flat because of her almost daily phone conversations with a network of friends from Estonia (her native country), and because she

was able to recreate the special atmosphere of her previous home of 20 years with a large collection of Estonian textiles, carpets, and handicrafts. (pp. 107–108)

Another strategy for retaining and nurturing meaning through place involves retaining links with former environments and maintaining continuity with past settings (Rowles, 1979). Too often, there is a tendency to assume that severance from a familiar setting should be absolute, a clean break in order to minimize separation anxiety. We suggest that this may be precisely the wrong strategy. Instead, there is strong evidence that retaining and enhancing as many links to past places as possible will bring significant benefits. In some cases it is possible to periodically return for visits to former environments. In other situations, visitors who still reside in the former setting can provide an ongoing link with the places from which the individual has departed. And in situations where physical return to former settings is not possible, their character and aura can be nurtured through shared reminiscence (Rowles, 1990). A proliferation of interest in the value of reminiscence groups and reminiscence therapy in long-term care institutional settings as a medium for connecting institutionalized residents with their pasts (and, by extension, with the places of their pasts) bodes well for the future of such approaches (Burnside, 1996; Haight, 1998; Hendricks, 1995; Rybarczyk & Bellg, 1997).

Conclusion

Meaning is an elusive concept. Ultimately, meaning can only be created and experienced by the self, albeit often in response to external stimuli and within a specific social context. Some people derive deep personal meaning from the smallest events in their lives. Others seem to skim across the waters of life barely touching the surface. Yet the experience of meaning, and the incidents in people's lives that provide sources of meaning, can be key elements in the formation and maintenance of personal identity and sense of self (Kaufman, 1986).

In this chapter, we have argued that one important source of meaning is a sense of place. We have argued that the ability to derive and sustain meaning, both through place-making and through the recollection and integration of the places of our lives within our persona, is a source of support and may be related to well-being in old age. In the artifacts we accumulate and the places we possess (even if only in our consciousness) we define who we are.

We do not contend that all people experience the places of their lives in the same way. For some, the very core of their being may be bound up in place. For others, place is little more than space, the medium of their existence; it carries little meaning. But while it is important to avoid overromanticized stereotyping of place attachment and the significance of the meaning of place, we would contend that in an increasingly mobile society where frequent relocation is the norm, there is a tendency to devalue the role of place in molding and reinforcing identity. As a society we are becoming increasingly alienated from place. Indeed, it has been argued that placelessness has become a predominant motif of contemporary life (Relph, 1976). Yet if, as philosophers and ethologists alike have argued, attachment and a sense of rootedness is a fundamental component of being human, our alienation from place is surely not without cost. What do we give up when we ignore what may be an elemental need for bonding with the places of our lives? In particular, with respect both to the way in which we treat our elders and to our own experience of aging, to what extent are we reducing the quality of life by undervaluing, if not completely ignoring, the role of places as sources of meaning?

Aldrich, C., & Mendkoff, C. (1963). Relocation of the aged and disabled: A mortality study. *Journal of the American Geriatrics Society, 11*(3), 183–194.

Altman, I., & Werner, C. M. (Eds.). (1985). *Home environments.* New York: Plenum Press.

American Association of Retired Persons/Administration on Aging. (1989). *A profile of older Americans.* Washington DC: Author.

Ardrey, R. (1966). *The territorial imperative: A personal inquiry into the animal origins of property and nations.* New York: Atheneum.

Bachelard, G. (1994). *The poetics of space.* (Marie Jolas, Trans.). Boston: Beacon Press. (Original work published 1957)

Barker, R. G. (1968). *Ecological psychology.* Stanford, CA: Stanford University Press.

Barker, R. G., & Barker, L. S. (1961). The psychological ecology of old people in Midwest, Kansas, and Yoredale, Yorkshire. *Journal of Gerontology, 61,* 231–239.

Belk, R. W. (1992). Attachment to possessions. In I. Altman & S. M. Lowe (Eds.), *Place attachment* (pp. 37–62). New York: Plenum Press.

Boschetti, M. A. (1985). *The older person's attachment to the physical environment of the residential setting.* Unpublished Ph.D. dissertation. Ann Arbor, MI: University Microfilms.

Boschetti, M. A. (1990). Reflections on home: Implications for housing design for elderly persons. *Housing and Society, 17*(3), 57–65.

Boschetti, M. A. (1995). Attachment to personal possessions: An interpretive study of the older person's experiences. *Journal of Interior Design, 21*(1), 1–12.

Brown, B. B., & Perkins, D. D. (1992). Disruptions in place attachment. In I. Altman & S. M. Low (Eds.), *Place attachment* (pp. 279–304). New York: Plenum Press.

Burnside, R. N. (1996). Life review and reminiscence in nursing practice. In J. E. Birren, G. M. Kenyon, J. Ruth, J. J. F. Schroots & T. Svensson (Eds.), *Aging and biography: Explorations in adult development* (pp. 248–264). New York: Springer.

Buttimer, A. (1980). Home, reach, and the sense of place. In A. Buttimer & D. Seamon (Eds.), *The human experience of space and place* (pp. 166–187). New York: St. Martin's Press.

Callahan, J. J. (1992). Aging in place. *Generations, 16,* 5–6.

Carp, F. M. (1966). *A future for the aged.* Austin: University of Texas Press.

Chawla, L. (1992). Childhood place attachments. In I. Altman & S. M. Low (Eds.), *Place attachment* (pp. 63–86). New York: Plenum Press.

Clark, W. A. V., & Davies, S. (1990). Elderly mobility and mobility outcomes. *Research on Aging, 12*(4), 430–462.

Csikszentmihalyi, M., & Rochberg-Halton, E. (1981). *The meaning of things: Domestic symbols and the self.* Chicago: University of Chicago Press.

Cuba, L. (1989). From visitor to resident: Retiring in vacationland. *Generations, 13,* 63–67.

Cuba, L., & Hummon, D. M. (1993). A place to call home: Identification with dwelling, community and region. *Sociological Quarterly, 34*(1), 111–131.

Cuba, L., & Longino, C. F., Jr. (1991). Regional retirement migration: The case of Cape Cod. *Journal of Gerontology, 46*(1), S33–42.

Cutchin, M. P. (1997a). Community and self: Concepts for rural physician integration and retention. *Social Science and Medicine, 44,* 1661–1674.

Cutchin, M. P. (1997b). Physician retention in rural communities: The perspective of experiential place integration. *Health and Place, 3,* 25–41.

Danermark, B., & Ekstrom, M. (1990). Relocation and health effects on the elderly: A commented research review. *Journal of Sociology and Social Welfare, 17*(1), 25–49.

Detzner, D. F., Bell, L., & Stum, M. (1991). The meaning of home and possessions to elderly public housing residents displaced by fire. *Housing and Society, 18*(2), 3–12.

Dickinson, D. (1996). Can elderly residents with memory problems be prepared for relocation? *Journal of Clinical Nursing, 5*(2), 99–104.

Dovey, K. (1985). Home and Homelessness. In I. Altman & C. M. Werner (Eds.), *Home environments* (pp. 33–64.) New York: Plenum Press.

Eliade, M. (1959). *The sacred and the profane.* New York: Harcourt, Brace.

Fogel, B. S. (1992). Psychological aspects of staying at home. *Generations, 16*(2), 15–19.

Fried, M. (1963). Grieving for a lost home. In L. J. Duhl (Ed.). *The urban condition* (pp. 151–171). New York: Basic Books.

Gans, H. J. (1962). *The urban villagers.* New York: Free Press.

Gittel, R., & Vidal, A.. (1998). *Community organizing: Building social capital as a development strategy.* Thousand Oaks, CA: Sage.

Golant, S. M. (1992). *Housing America's elderly: Many possibilities, few choices.* Newbury Park, CA: Sage.

Gubrium, J. F. (1993). *Speaking of life: Horizons of meaning for nursing home residents.* New York: Aldine De Gruyter.

Haas, W. H. (1990). Retirement migration: Boon or burden? *Journal of Applied Gerontology, 9*(4), 387–463.

Haight, B. K., Michel, Y., & Hendrix, S. (1998). Life review: Preventing despair in newly relocated nursing home residents; short and long term effects. *International Journal of Aging and Human Development, 47*(2), 119–142.

Halperin, R. H. (1998). *Practicing community: Class, culture and power in an urban neighborhood.* Austin: University of Texas Press.

Hart, R. (1979). *Children's experience of place.* New York: Irvington.

Hartwigsen, G. (1987). Older widows and the transference of home. *International Journal of Aging and Human Development, 25*(3), 195–207.

Hendricks, J. (Ed.). (1995). *The meaning of reminiscence and life review.* Amityville, New York: Baywood.

Horowitz, M. J., & Schulz, R. (1983). The relocation controversy: Criticism and commentary on five recent studies. *Gerontologist, 23*(3), 229–234.

Howell, S. C. (1983). The meaning of place in old age. In G. D. Rowles & R. J. Ohta (Eds.), *Aging and milieu: Environmental perspectives on growing old* (pp. 97–107). New York: Academic Press.

Hummon, D. M. (1990). *Commonplaces: Community ideology and identity in American culture.* Albany: State University Press of New York.

Hunt, M. E., & Pastalan, L. A. (1987). Easing relocation: An environmental learning process. In V. Regnier & J. Pynoos (Eds.), *Housing the aged: Design directives and policy considerations* (pp. 421–440). New York: Elsevier.

Jacobs, J. (1961). *The death and life of great American cities.* New York: Vintage Books.

Kaufman, S. R. (1986). *The ageless self: Sources of meaning in late life.* Madison: University of Wisconsin Press.

Keller, S. (1969). *The urban neighborhood: A sociological perspective.* New York: Random House.

Kemper, P., & Murtaugh, C. M. (1991). Lifetime use of nursing home care. *New England Journal of Medicine, 324*(9), 595–600.

Kielhofner, G. (1995). Habituation subsystem. In G. Keilhofner (Ed.), *A model of human occupation: Theory and application* (2nd ed., pp. 63–81). Baltimore: Williams & Wilkins.

Lawton, M. P. (1990). Knowledge resources and gaps in housing the aged. In D. Tilson (Ed.). *Aging in place* (pp. 287–309). Glenview, IL: Scott, Foresman.

Lawton, M. P. (1998). Environment and aging: Theory revisited. In R. J. Scheidt & P. G. Windley (Eds.), *Environment and aging theory: A focus on housing* (pp. 1–32). Westport, CT: Greenwood Press.

Litwak, E., & Longino, C. F., Jr. (1987). Migration patterns among the elderly: A developmental perspective. *Gerontologist, 27,* 266–272.

Longino, C. F. (1995). *Retirement migration in America.* Houston, TX: Vacation Publications.

Ludwig, F. M. (1997). How routine facilitates wellbeing in older women. *Occupational Therapy International, 4*(3), 213–228.

Marcus, C. C. (1992). Environmental memories. In I. Altman & S. M. Low (Eds.), *Place attachment* (pp. 87–112). New York: Plenum Press.

McCracken, A. (1987). Emotional impact of possession loss. *Journal of Gerontological Nursing, 13*(2), 14–19.

McHugh, K. E., & Mings, R. C. (1996). The circle of migration: Attachment to place in aging. *Annals of the Association of American Geographers, 86*(3), 530–550.

Morris, B. R. (1992). Reducing inventory: Divestiture of personal possessions. *Journal of Women and Aging, 4*(2), 79–92.

Norris-Baker, C. (1998). The evolving concept of behavior settings: Implications for housing older adults. In R. J. Scheidt & P. G. Windley (Eds.), *Environment and aging theory: A focus on housing* (pp. 141–160). Westport, CT: Greenwood Press.

Norris-Baker, C. (1999). Aging on the old frontier and the new: A behavior setting approach to the declining small towns of the midwest. *Environment and Behavior 31*(2), 240–258.

Norris-Baker, C., & Scheidt, R. J. (1991). A contextual approach to serving older residents of economically-threatened small towns. *Journal of Aging Studies, 5,* 333–346.

Norris-Baker, C., & Scheidt, R. J. (1994). From "Our Town" to "Ghost Town"? The changing context of home for rural elders. *International Journal of Aging and Human Development, 38,* 181–202.

O'Bryant, S. L. (1982). The value of home to older persons. *Research on Aging, 4,* 349–363.

O'Bryant, S. L. (1983). The subjective value of home to older home owners. *Journal of Housing for the Elderly, 1,* 29–43.

Pastalan, L. A., Davis, L. F., & Haberkorn, S. B. (1975). *Pennsylvania nursing home relocation program*. Ann Arbor, MI: University of Michigan Press.

Paton, H., & Cram, F. (1992). Personal possessions and environmental control: The experiences of elderly women in three residential settings. *Journal of Women and Aging, 4*(2), 61–78.

Pynoos, J. (1990). Public policy and aging in place: Identifying the problems and potential solutions. In D. Tilson (Ed.), *Aging in place: Supporting the frail elderly in residential environments* (pp. 167–208). Glenview, IL: Scott, Foresman.

Relph, E. (1976). *Place and placelessness*. London: Pion Limited.

Rowles, G. D. (1978). *Prisoners of space? Exploring the geographical experience of older people*. Boulder, CO: Westview Press.

Rowles, G. D. (1979). The last new home: Facilitating the older person's adjustment to institutional space. In S. M. Golant (Ed.), *Location and environment of the elderly population* (pp. 81–94). New York: Wiley.

Rowles, G. D. (1980). Toward a geography of growing old. In A. Buttimer & D. Seamon (Eds.), *The human experience of space and place* (pp. 55–72). London: Croom Helm.

Rowles, G. D. (1981). The surveillance zone as meaningful space for the aged. *The Gerontologist, 21*(3), 304–311.

Rowles, G. D. (1983a). Between worlds: A relocation dilemma for the Appalachian elderly. *International Journal of Aging and Human Development, 17*(4), 301–314.

Rowles, G. D. (1983b). Place and personal identity in old age: Observations from Appalachia. *Journal of Environmental Psychology, 3,* 299–313.

Rowles, G. D. (1990). Place attachment among the small town elderly. *Journal of Rural Community Psychology, 11,* 103–120.

Rowles, G. D. (1991). Beyond performance: Being in place as a component of occupational therapy. *American Journal of Occupational Therapy, 45*(3), 265–271.

Rowles, G. D. (1993). Evolving images of place in aging and "Aging in Place." *Generations, 17*(2), 65–70.

Rowles, G. D., & Watkins, J. F. (1993). Elderly migration and development in small communities. *Growth and Change, 24*(4), 509–538.

Rubinstein, R. L. (1987). The significance of personal objects to older people. *Journal of Aging Studies, 1*(3), 225–238.

Rubinstein, R. L. (1989). The home environments of older people: A description of the psychosocial processes linking person to place. *Journal of Gerontology, 44*, S45–S53.

Rubinstein, R. L. (1990). Personal identity and environmental meaning in later life. *Journal of Aging Studies, 4*(2), 131–147.

Rubinstein, R. L., & Parmelee, P. A. (1992). Attachment to place and the representation of the life course by the elderly. In I. Altman & S. M. Low (Eds.), *Place attachment* (pp. 139–163). New York: Plenum Press.

Rybarczyk, B., & Bellg, A. (1997). *Listening to life stories: A new approach to stress intervention in health care.* New York: Springer.

Scheidt, R. J. (1993). Place and personality in adult development. In R. Kastenbaum (Ed.), *Encyclopedia of adult development* (pp. 370–377). Phoenix: Oryx Press.

Scheidt, R. J., & Norris-Baker, C. (1990). A transactional approach to environmental stress among older residents of rural communities. *Journal of Rural Community Psychology, 11*, 5–30.

Scheidt, R. J., & Norris-Baker, L. (1993). The environmental context of poverty among older residents of economically endangered Kansas towns. *Journal of Applied Gerontology, 12*(3), 335–348.

Scheidt, R. J., & Norris-Baker, L. (1999). Place therapies for older adults: Conceptual and interventive approaches. *International Journal of Aging and Human Development, 48*(1), 1–15.

Seamon, D. (1979). *A geography of the lifeworld: Movement, rest and encounter.* New York: St. Martin's Press.

Seamon, D. (1980). Body subject, time-space routines, and place ballets. In A. Buttimer & D. Seamon (Eds.), *The human experience of space and place* (pp. 148–165). London: Croom Helm.

Seamon, D., & Nordin, C. (1980). Marketplace as place ballet: A Swedish example. *Landscape, 24*(3), 35–41.

Serow, W. J., & Charity, D. A. (1988). Return migration of the elderly in the United States: Recent trends. *Research on Aging, 10*(2), 155–168.

Shumaker, S. A., & Conti, G. J. (1985). Understanding mobility in America: Conflicts between stability and change. In I. Altman & C. M. Werner (Eds.), *Home environments* (pp. 237–253). New York: Plenum Press.

Strahan, G. (1987). Nursing home characteristics: Preliminary data from the 1985 National Nursing Home Survey. *NCHS Advancedata, 131*, 1–7.

Suttles, G. (1968). *The social order of the slum: Ethnicity and territory in the inner city.* Chicago: University of Chicago Press.

Tilson, D. (Ed.). (1990). *Aging in place: Supporting the frail elderly in residential environments.* Glenview, IL: Scott, Foresman.

Wapner, S., Demick, J., & Redondo, J. P. (1990). Cherished possessions and adaptation of older people to nursing homes. *International Journal of Aging and Human Development, 31*(3), 219–235.

Wheeler, W. M. (1995). *Elderly residential experience: The evolution of places as residence.* New York: Garland.

White, S. E. (1987). Return migration to eastern Kentucky and the stem family concept. *Growth and Change, 18*(2), 38–52.

Wiseman, R. F., & Roseman, C. C. (1979). A typology of elderly migration based on the decision making process. *Economic Geography, 55*(4), 324–337.

Young, H. M. (1998). Moving to congregate housing: The last chosen home. *Journal of Aging Studies, 12*(2), 149–165.

SIX

Bringers of Allah: The Druse Elders

David Gutmann

EDITORS' INTRODUCTION Two different, though related, issues of meaning are, first, what meanings people give to values and goals and, second, what meanings people give to each other. Gutmann attends to the latter issue. More specifically, he is concerned with how someone who has moved beyond responsibilities for work and family can continue to be socially valued.

Gutmann says that whether an older person matters socially depends on whether he or she can contribute to a socially important enterprise. Some older people are able to do this here in America. They hold senior positions in institutions in which tradition is valued: our military, our judiciary, and many of our largest commercial institutions. The retired CEO, a member of the governing board, may be looked to for the assessment of current policies against the experience of the past; for memories of the way things were done in the past, what worked and what didn't, and what the founders of the enterprise intended; in short, for perspective and wisdom. Gutmann says that what happens in America only in certain sectors can in other places happen for the entire society. His example is the Druse.

Gutmann describes a society in which older men who have won the respect of the community through their behavior in earlier life are inducted into roles as spiritual leaders. They are taught the unwritten spiritual understandings of their community and become the repository of the community's spiritual beliefs. They join the elders who are the community's sole link to its spiritual heritage.

Gutmann proposes that for there to be roles such as those provided by the Druse to respected older men, the society must have needs whose fulfillment can utilize the special characteristics of the older person. Older men, Gutmann says, have retreated from the active and often aggressive outlook of their earlier selves toward a more contemplative, more passive, outlook. He bases his view on research he has done in many societies in which he has shown that men become more receptive, less given to domination, as they enter later life. Compatible with their changed selves are roles that require probity, patience, and wisdom, as these are defined in the society, rather than the more assertive masculine virtues that are likely to have been on view in the men's earlier lives.

Gutmann revisits the theory of later-life disengagement, a theory that has been attacked as untrue and subtly disparaging but that continues to have adherents. One argument for the theory was Gutmann's own finding that active striving diminished in later life. But Gutmann says that his finding is misused by those who conclude from it that disengagement is a normal developmental event of later life. He says that active striving is not essential to social contribution. The Druse show one way this is the case, and the institutions of our society that value older participants show still other ways.

One problem in the American way of doing things, Gutmann says, is that we celebrate the young and, often, the rebellious, at the expense of those who represent continuity with the past. Doing so has freed us to embrace change and the new, but it has cost us dearly by bringing an indifference to tradition and, with it, uncertainty regarding values and goals. For Gutmann, failing to recognize how capable our grandparents can be in giving us direction leaves our society adrift. By denying our elderly roles in which they can continue to contribute, we deny ourselves the benefit of their unique capacity to strengthen the foundations of our society.

The despairing view of the aged regards them as leading lives deprived of significance, starved of meaning. No longer engaged with the productive and reproductive concerns that once gave fiber and significance to their lives, they are fated either to fill their emptiness with the trivial pleasures of couch potatoes or to succumb to the three Ds: depression, dementia, and death.

There is some truth to this bleak picture: enough to provide gainful employment to legions of gerontological counselors and social workers. But it is not a universal truth. It does not apply to a sizable portion of elders—not in this society, nor in humankind as a whole.

Professional subcultures in institutions of our own society are often gerontocracies: for example, the military, the priesthood, and branches of medicine and academia. They are governed by former practitioners who persevere, from their positions of leadership, in representing the ideological underpinnings and the ethical rules of the enterprise.

The elders who guide our institutions are not passively waiting for their lives to be given meaning by Elderhostels or by grandchildren; quite the contrary, they are the purveyors of significance for the younger practitioners. It is they who remind cadets of the traditions that underlie practice, of the heroic founders whose virtues are crystallized in these traditions, and of the ideals the traditions embody.

Nor are the elders of our own institutions unusual in their role. In general, where core values, rituals, and practices derive from founding legends, those having to do with divine intervention into human affairs, we find the rule of the elder. As Leo Simmons (1945) reports, the traditional elders of preliterate groups, as they withdraw from intensive involvement with physical challenges, tend to become the interpreters and administrators of the moral sector of society. Within the ordinary world, they become the norm-bearers, the setters of standards; they are in addition the bridgeheads to the unordinary, to the gods, to the entities of highest significance. The young adults take care of daily matters, the workings of the pragmatic society, while the traditional elders tend culture in its more numinous, enduring, meaning-providing aspects.

Nature and Nurture in the Aging Male

In this essay, I discuss the Druse of the Levant, a paradigmatic clerical and gerontocratic society whose unique culture is founded on the bridgehead, meaning-imparting functions of their elders. The nature versus nurture issue is perhaps the central question in the behavioral sciences and cannot be put to rest by a single study. Nevertheless, the case of the Highland Druse of the Levant suggests an integrating model: it suggests that a society's somewhat arbitrary age-graded role requirements can act together with the universal developmental potentials of later life to bring about a meaning-dense and enriching life for the traditional elder.

Men driven by newly emergent internal dynamisms can find guides to socially acceptable behavior in the cultural protocols provided by their social habitats. Covert, universal drives do not make men less sensitive to overt social influences but rather steer them toward suitable social norms, understandings, and possibilities. Thus, younger men might recognize the existence of a religious tradition in their society and be knowledgeable about its precepts, but their subjective relation to that tradition would differ from that of their fathers. The younger men could report—as anthropological informants, for example—on the rules of the religious tradition, but they might not refer to these codes for regulation of their behavior. By the same token, the aging fathers of these young men would know a good deal about the usages that governed the productive life in their society but would find them less personally relevant than those that organized the religious life and the relationship to God. Thus, owing to the influence of emerging developmental dispositions and sensitivities, older men would make real for themselves social norms and conventions that had far less impact for them when they were younger.

My research, of which my studies of the Druse are a part, has been directed to understanding the developmental psychology of aging. My guiding hypothesis has been that important psychological orientations, formed around particular mixes of passivity and aggressivity and of dependence and autonomy, would discriminate age groups within culturally homogeneous societies. In particular, younger men across cultures could be anticipated to reveal motives, attitudes, and images characteristic of an active, production-centered, and competitive stance, while older men could be anticipated to show the reverse pattern. Older men would give priority to community over agency, to receptivity over productivity, to mildness and humility over competition.

The Druse elders have high prestige. If, despite their high prestige, the Druse elders are like elders elsewhere, in that they show a response to challenge that is more nearly passive than that of the younger men of their society, the change can be ascribed to intrapsychic—possibly developmental—rather than extrinsic, situational influences. Accordingly, along with the Navajo and the Mexican Maya, the Druse, as a paradigm gerontocracy, were added to the sample of culturally and ethnically varied societies selected to test the developmental hypothesis.

As an unexpected finding, the Druse revealed a central paradox of their gerontocratic society: ego states that have become more passive with aging can be lived out, with positive consequences for self and society, in the special social roles available to traditional men. In the balance of this essay, I look at the ways the universal psychological developments of later life, in concert with unique Druse lifeways, demographics, and culture, lead to this outcome.

The Druse People and Their Elders

The villages of the Druse, usually sited for defense on hilltops or mountainsides, are scattered through the highland regions of Lebanon, Syria, and Galilean Israel. The Druse people are mainly agriculturists, cultivating fruits, olives, wheat, and tobacco. They speak Arabic, and their lifeways are in most respects similar to those of the patriarchal Muslim villagers of the Levant.

Over eight hundred years ago the Druse chose minority status, on religious grounds, within the larger Arab world. The first Druse broke with the Muslim religion on doctrinal points and thereby let themselves in for the legion of troubles that go with self-chosen heretical status. Over the years the Druse have suffered much religious persecution at the hands of the Muslim majority, and they have developed the personal and cultural traits that generally characterize a minority that has managed to survive in the face of daunting odds. Since they could not take the good will of the majority for granted, they have learned as a group mainly to trust themselves—to rely on the courage, strength, and wit of the Druse people. Albeit grudgingly, their neighbors have acknowledged these virtues: throughout their history, individual Druse have been prominent in the political and particularly the military affairs of the Middle East.

Each individual Druse man tends to reproduce in his personality the general stance of the culture. Thus, Druse men are fiercely self-reliant and depend chiefly on themselves or on resources that they alone have cultivated: the produce of their fields or the strength of their sons. In effect, they trust very little what comes from outside of themselves as gift or gratuity.

The Druse men's mistrust of that which is not under self-control extends to their mental life. Accordingly, they are extremely stubborn and refractory as individuals, not only against coercion from others' will but against coercion from their own willfulness, their own spontaneous emotions. Thus, they do not allow themselves to become excited; even illiterate Druse peasants give priority to rationality over emotionality. In effect, they value the mental resource that they have created for themselves over the raw emotions that have been "foisted" on them by the body and its urgent appetites.

As part of their self-reliance, Druse men must deny any needfulness and must hold themselves in the position of the giver, rather than the receiver. Thus, they are unfailingly and sometimes even aggressively hospitable. Moreover, the harshest Druse insult is to call another man a "hotel-keeper," implying that he charges his guests for his hospitality.

A major political problem for Druse men is the coordination of their own community life, centered as it is around their religion, with the requirements and demands of the non-Druse majority, which has frequently been hostile to their faith. Over the centuries the Druse have learned to blend flexibility and accommodation with firmness and, in matters of tradition, rigidity. They change and compromise in minor ways which do not touch on the core of their religious tradition, in order to maintain that same core inviolate and unchanged. Thus, as in Israel, they typically offer their sons to be career soldiers and policemen for the majority government—in effect, they trade military service for political security. But while the Druse are usually meticulously observant of the secular law, they will not tolerate any violation by the non-Druse majority of the core of their religion or their traditions. They will not, for example, tolerate any attack on the honor of their women or their priests. If compliance does not succeed in staving off dishonor and sacrilege, then the Druse will, almost to the last man, go to war.

Though their villages have always been scattered over different countries, the Druse say of themselves that they are like a large brass plate: "Strike one corner, then the whole will vibrate." True to this motto, the Druse led the post–World War I revolution against the French, which gave rise to the establishment of modern Syria. They are famous throughout the Middle East for their ardor in battle.

The Druse Age-Grade System

Since the Druse people comprise a religious sect, their religion is central to the workings of their society and to the sense of individual Druse identity. Nevertheless, it is kept secret, not only from the outside world but also from the younger people of the community. The Druse have learned to treat their heretic religion as a kind of conspiracy within the body of Islam. Therefore, the younger Druse—who might unthinkingly reveal their identity to non-Druse neighbors—were in times past not instructed in the religion or even told that they were Druse until they arrived at the age of discretion.

The tradition of keeping the religion secret from the younger members of the community survives even to these more liberal times. Thus, younger Druse men, those not yet initiated to the secret books, are called Jahil, the "unknowing" ones. Those older men who have been accepted into the religious society and who have received their copy of the secret text are known as Aqil: literally, those who "know."

The strict criteria that govern admission to the inner circles of the Druse religion also determine the age-grade systems, the social norms, and the shared understandings that partially govern the latter half of life for the typical Druse male. In the more traditional villages some men might become Aqil in early middle age, after they have established their family of procreation; and there are even a few Aqil youths, seminary-trained sons of famous religious leaders. A few secular-minded holdouts, as well as poor men (those who cannot afford an open, hospitable house) are not called to Aqil-hood. But in general, most traditional men, those who have led exemplary "householder's" lives, are invited to become Aqil in late middle age, usually after their children have left the parental home.

As noted earlier, Druse men of any age are generally formal and punctilious, but this manner intensifies after a man becomes Aqil. He also receives increased deference, both within the family—where he reigns as the "Allah of the family"—and in the public square. Signaling his new status, the Aqil shaves his scalp and adopts special garb, including the Lhafi, the traditional white and red fez. In keeping with such priestly garb, he becomes the very model of stern propriety. The newly minted Aqil also gives up alcohol and tobacco, and spends much time in the Hilweh—the house of prayer—with other devout men. But the Aqil does not withdraw completely from pragmatic affairs into the Hilweh. Usually he continues his agricultural work, though more often as a supervisor of his grown sons than as a worker in the field. In addition, he is expected to be unfailingly hospitable, to seek hospitality at other respectable houses, and to appear at all important public functions.

Not only the outward dress and behavior, but also the inner life of the Aqil comes under strict control: he is expected to devote himself to good and pious thoughts and to renounce the errors, stupidities, and gross appetites of which he may have been guilty before being introduced to the true knowledge of Allah. It is therefore often difficult to interview an old Aqil concerning his childhood experiences. He becomes remote or evasive, even angry: "Why do you ask me about the time when I was ignorant, before I knew God? I was like an animal then, I did not think of God, and it is a shame to remember such things!"

In sum, the Aqil purge themselves, consciously at least, of the appetites—and even the memories of the appetites—which violate the strict prescriptions of the religious life. Thus, as the typical Druse man passes into late middle life and old age he appears to shunt onto the behavioral and attitudinal tracks that have been prepared for him by the age-grade systems of Druse society. His life appears to be almost completely governed by parochial customs, of the sort that have meaning only to the religious Druse.

But the self-regulating Aqil also set the controlling social and moral rhythms for their community as a whole. I do not know if the Aqil meet in formal councils to make and disseminate policy within individual villages. My sense is that daily meetings of pious men—meetings that I could never observe— are the settings for policy deliberations, as well as for prayer, and that the decisions made in the house of worship are communicated, Aqil to Aqil and Aqil to Jahil, in the daily round of visits.

However they acquire their power, the Aqil clearly are able to enforce their writ. Receiving you in their homes, individual Aqil can be jolly and welcoming; but when they appear in the aggregate, as at public ceremonial functions, they form an intimidating moral mass, old men who radiate a sense of un-

challenged authority. Even an outsider like myself feels a mix-
ture of awe and uneasiness in their dark, silently reproachful
presence. Appearing together, the black-garbed Aqil become
the communal superego, with a human face. As such, the Aqil
remind the Jahil, within their daily lives, of Allah's awful
mercy. Through them, ordinary observances, the daily mo-
tions of conformity are converted to ritual, to the service of
Allah. Freighted with such powerful meanings, the hard disciplines required by Druse society are made pleasurable; more
to the point, they become the foundations of individual identity and social stability.

I should note that I was forced by the Druse conspiracy of
silence to become a kind of academic Jahil: in order to preserve my legitimacy as a researcher, I had to make a defensive
show of my ignorance about Druse theology and religious
culture. While I was free to push my enquiry into the individual psychology of Druse men, including the Aqil, I had to
carefully avoid direct questions about the details of Druse religion or about the lifeways of the Aqil who exemplify it. Therefore, while the following account has some psychological
depth, as a report on the social organization and activities of
the Aqil it is necessarily limited and impressionistic. However,
I believe that my interviews, though deficient in theological
and, to a lesser extent, sociological, detail, do make evident
the weighty presence of the Aqil, a unique religious gerontocracy, in the daily life of the Druse villages.

Universal Trends in Druse Aging

I asked the Druse elders whom I interviewed to interpret the
ambiguous pictures of the Thematic Apperception Test (TAT)
battery. The projective data they provided suggest that the
inner, subjective life of Druse elders changes in later years in

step with universal developments as well as with extrinsic, parochial constraints.

The data indicate a pattern of psychological changes that is in conformity with those observed in their age peers from radically different cultures, where older men do not necessarily enter a rigorous religious subculture (see Gutmann, 1994). The comparative analysis of the longitudinal projective and interview materials reveals that, like their age-peers in other societies, older Druse turn away from Active Mastery orientations, which feature an aggressive engagement with the physical and social worlds, toward more compliant and dependent Passive Mastery orientations.

For example, when we examine Druse interpretations of the "rope climber" card of the TAT, which pictures a seminude, muscular man either climbing or descending a rope, we find that the interpretations change, with age, along the predicted trajectories. Younger Druse men see the climber ascending the rope, for productive and/or competitive purposes. In contrast, older Druse men—including many Aqil—interpret the picture as portraying a more easy-going, even passive man: he is descending the rope, he is swinging on it playfully, or he is fleeing from a fire. (Such "fire" themes portray vital energy as dangerous and alien to the familiar self; the climber escapes from it as from a dangerous thing.)

These and other Druse age-linked distributions of themes roughly parallel the distributions of themes provided by men in other subsistence-level peasant societies of my crosscultural sample: the Navajo, as well as the Highland and Lowland Maya. Given the privileged social position of the Druse elders, and given that their health is generally sound, the shift from Active Mastery to Passive Mastery is not reactive to a bad physical or social situation. Rather, it expresses universal developments of later life, possibly the generic male response to the phasing out of parental responsibilities (see Gutmann, 1994).

The Social and the Personal
in Druse Religious Life

The passive leanings that emerge openly in the TAT protocols of elderly Druse appear to be universally displayed by elderly men. However, the question of their force remains: are the leanings powerful enough to dictate overt behavior?

As noted earlier, the public behavior of the older Aqil seems to be completely ordered by his local culture and not by some species-wide undertow toward passivity. When we look at the conventional behavior of the religious Druse man, we find him going busily from place to place, from one ceremonial visit to another, praying or receiving guests with elaborate hospitality. In his social relations he is not submissive but rather dogmatic and dictatorial, laying down the law to his younger relations. Within the framework of the religious life, the older Aqil seems to behave in an active rather than a passive fashion.

Thus, when we ask the Aqil what he does as an observant man, he describes an energetic life. However, when we ask him about the meaning that the religious life holds for him—when we ask about his subjective relation to the religious life and to Allah—we get a different picture. It is at this level that the passive yearnings inferred from the TAT seem to make their appearance. When the Aqil talk about their relationship to Allah, fierce, patriarchal old Druse, still domineering toward their grown sons, will adopt completely the posture and the tone of the passive, self-effacing supplicant: "Allah is all and I am nothing; I live only in his will, and by his will. . . . I do not question his will. . . . I do not complain about my illness, because this is from God; and to complain about my illness is to question God." In his behavior as religious figure the Aqil resembles not only his Druse coreligionists but also his overtly passive age-peers in other societies.

Incidentally, these older men are not playing back, by rote, some prescription for conventional religious behavior. Depending on their age, the Aqil seem to interpret their religious responsibilities differently. Thus, when we asked one of the few young Aqil about the meaning for him of the religious life, he told us that his task was to seek out sinners, to correct their ways, and through such action to make the village acceptable in the eyes of God. In effect, the younger Aqil are social workers for God; their relationship to Allah is mediated by their aggressive action in his service. They define their responsibilities as something like cleaning up Dodge City. It is only among the old Aqil that we get the sense of a direct and personal relation to Allah, mediated not by work in the sinful world but by supplication and prayer. Their job is not to purify the village but to cleanse themselves. Allah is for them an intensely felt and loving presence: as they talk of God their eyes shine, and the voices of these old patriarchs tremble with emotion. They become not unlike the stereotype of a submissive woman speaking fearfully and yearningly of her masterful male partner.

There are no rules, explicit or implicit, in Druse society that tell young Aqil to relate to Allah through their own active initiatives, or for older men to have a relationship that is centered on the power and actions of that same Allah. Clearly, there is a range of permissible postures toward Allah available to the Druse, regardless of age, but each age-cohort finds certain postures more congenial than others. The younger Aqil define a relationship to Allah that is in conformity with the principles of Active Mastery, while older Aqil enact the themes of Passive Mastery. These age preferences reflect intrinsic definitions of self and surround rather than social coercion.

The religious sector provides a setting in which fantasy and reality are commingled, a world in which dreams—concretized into icons and totems—enter the real world. The religious attachment of the Aqil allows the passive strivings noted in the older man's TAT-sponsored fantasies to find their overt, dramatic expression. The world of faith provides the Aqil the scope within which to achieve a virtual reality that matches his needs.

The example given here illustrates the relatively seamless fit that often exists between particular roles and developmental potentials in the traditional community. As I have shown, the older Druse shares with his age peers in other societies a tendency toward androgyny in later life. However, in his case he does not need to make some final and conflictual choice between active and passive, or between "masculine" and "feminine" ways of relating. The religious sector of his society provides him with a separate psychosocial niche in which he can live out passive and covertly "feminine" strivings, even as he continues to act in a domineering fashion towards his sons, to rule his extended family, and to influence community policy in the "real" world. Thus, the religious role requires and gives high significance to those psychic potentials which are released by the older man's withdrawal from the active tasks of parenthood and production. The yearnings that men in secular societies might find uncomfortable, or attempt to disown, perhaps with neurotic or psychosomatic symptoms as a consequence, the old traditional Druse experiences as his worshipful linkage to God.

Passivity and Power

While the religious role suits the special needs of older men, their leanings toward mildness and accommodation are equally fitted to the requirements of the religious role. In the preliterate mind, life-sustaining vitality or power does not originate in the mundane, everyday world. Life-sustaining power has its ultimate origin in supernatural, extracommunal sources: in the spirits of ancestral dead, in totemic animals, and particularly in the gods. The particular source of power varies by cultural prescription, but the idea that the prosaic world owes its substance and vitality to power imported from the supernatural is general across traditional worlds.

Wherever this worldview is institutionalized, specially anointed figures are required to station themselves on the interface between the mundane and supernatural worlds so as to "attract" the benevolent aspect of supernatural power, to contain it, and to make it available to the life forms of the community and its ecosystem (see Gutmann, 1973). The old man's emerging humility and submissiveness fits him to live on the dangerous interface between the gods and the mundane community, and, through his prayers, to bring life-sustaining forces into the world so as to maintain and increase children, flocks, and crops. Through him, the world becomes vivid with the aura of the gods. The passivity that could lead to vulnerability, depression, and psychosomatic illness in other settings becomes in these settings—of which the traditional Druse society is one—the very core and pivot of the older man's social prestige and personal identity.

Disengagement or Reengagement?

The theory of later-life disengagement put forward by Cumming and Henry (1961) was for a while the reigning conception in the social psychology of aging, and it still has adherents. In essence, it proposes a mutual disengagement: the agencies of society withdraw their attention from the aged; and, at the same time, the aged withdraw from society's normative restraints, becoming more idiosyncratic but also more "liberated." Though the theory was developed exclusively from

United States urban studies and was not tested crossculturally, its authors claimed that disengagement is both mandatory and universal—a developmental event. In their view the older person who sets out to oppose this dictate of nature is fighting a losing battle and is asking for psychological trouble.

In part, Cumming and Henry justified their case for disengagement as a developmental (hence universal) phenomenon by relating this process to another presumably developmental event: the emergence of passive ego states in the TAT protocols of their older male subjects. Since the age trend toward passive TAT imagery correlated with the age trend toward disengagement on other barometers in the study population, Cumming and Henry concluded that the two trends were linked into one inclusive developmental transition in which the increased passivity of later life represented the inner, subjective correlate of the total disengagement process.

The case of the Druse Aqil indicates that disengagement need not be compulsory. It even more strongly demonstrates that passivity is not inextricably tied to disengagement. Quite the contrary: in the Druse case—and probably in the case of other strongly religious folk societies—the so-called passivity of the older man can be the central, necessary component of his engagement with age-appropriate social roles, traditions, and associated normative controls.

Clearly, the older Druse Aqil switches his allegiance from the norms that govern the parental and productive life to those that dictate traditional and moral behavior, but in this transition he does not stray from the influence of normative controls as such. If anything, such controls gain increased influence over him. Although the older Druse may detach his interest and allegiance from those social codes that are no longer congenial to his passive needs, he does not detach himself from society per se, nor from its shared protocols. Rather, he links himself subjectively to the religious dimension of his culture and in so doing plays out, without shame, a core theme of Passive Mastery: the need to be in personal touch, as a supplicant, with a powerful, benevolent, and productive agency.

The Druse elder relinquishes his own productivity but not productivity per se. Instead of being the center of enterprise, he is now the bridge between the community and the productive, life-sustaining potencies of Allah. The old Aqil now carries forward the moral rather than the material work of the community. He is not starved for significance, nor is he a consumer of bestowed meanings; quite the contrary, his cohort stands in stubborn opposition to values and usages that come from outside Druse society and that in their eyes would be offensive to Allah.

Erik Erikson once said to me, "There is nothing destructive about deprivation per se. It is only deprivation without meaning that is psychologically destructive." In the Druse case, the Aqil import significance from Allah and export it into their world. In doing so, they provide the Jahil with meaning-laden reasons for tolerating the rigorous disciplines and the burdens of the heretic imposed by their sect and for deriving identity from these constraints.

Guided by needs and sensibilities that reflect his emerging passivity, the older Druse transits from one normative order to another within his society. In that transition he becomes, quite completely, the instrument and the representation of the traditional moral order that he has adopted and that has adopted him. He is not disengaged: he is, rather, reengaged.

What is true for the Druse is also in general true for the men of other tradition-oriented societies. The disengagement that Cumming and Henry found in our society does not extend to all versions of the human condition; indeed, it is the exception rather than the rule. In a more traditional society than ours it would be only the first step in a larger evolution, a transition whose movement toward its natural terminus of reengagement is too often interrupted or aborted in our secular society. It may well be that disengagement is only an artifact of those societies in which the old man has no traditional moral order that would foster his reengagement with his society once he has decoupled from those social norms that regulate the parental and productive life periods.

In sum, the movement among elderly men toward Passive and even Magical Mastery appears to be universal, but it does not necessarily lead to disengagement. The Druse case shows that the inexorable psychic developments of later life for men are not a necessary prelude to social withdrawal and physical death. Given a society that recognizes men's emerging dispositions, gives them potent significance, and articulates them into powerful offices, the so-called passivity of later life can provide the ground for a later life revival, for a kind of social rebirth of the male elder and for the refreshment of core cultural values for his society as a whole.

The American Way and the Druse Way

Our own American society has traveled along a radically different, even opposed, line of social evolution from that of the Druse. The founding myths and constitutive documents of our democracy proclaim a rebellion against the kind of clerical gerontocracy the Druse epitomize. Europe, under the arbitrary rule of princes and prelates, was the Old Country, the bad history that the new democracy would repeal.

There is no question that the major goals of the American anticlerical, antimonarchical, antigerontocratic revolutions have been achieved. A thick wall separates our churches from the workings of the secular state. Instead of monarchy we have celebrities: embodiments of dreams who dictate our fashions but generate no enduring policies or dynasties. Save for the relatively few pockets of gerontocracy in politics and professions referred to earlier, we have succeeded, as part of the continuing American revolution against gerontocracy, in turning elders into "the aged."

The American revolution continues: acting collectively, we have routinized drastic change and are on a continuous search-and-destroy mission against the remaining pockets of tradition—particularly those that derive from the patriarchal sectors of our heritage. But what we throw away, the Druse conserve. Seeing them as part of a sanctified way, the Druse gladly accept traditional, patriarchal disciplines. In Erikson's terms, the sacrifices that their traditions require of the Druse men have high meaning and so are not experienced as deprivation. Instead, they become a form of worship that puts observant Druse men, including the Jahil, in personal touch with the divine roots of their unique culture. For the Druse men, the restriction on appetite is a small price to pay for endowments of meaning that draw the sting from death.

Having weakened our traditions, we Americans have, as a side effect, undercut what is the major cultural route to finding significance in life: the sense of being in personal touch with some numinous order. With loss of this wellhead of significance, we weaken the connections between deprivation and meaning. We are hard put to find moral grounds for curbing any demand.

But the most troubling consequence is the unintended damage to those American age cohorts that are most advantaged among the Druse: the aged and the young. Gerontocrats are usually the bearers of tradition and the enforcers of traditional disciplines. We Americans deny to seniors the social and spiritual powers that, across the human range, they usually inherit.

Indeed, derogation of the older generation is an aspect of a national gerophobia that is reaching epidemic proportions as the "Baby Boom" generation enters its sixth decade. The gerophobia fuels growth industries of antiaging foods, drugs, exercise regimes, gurus, and self-help books all aimed at proving that aging can be overcome, life extended, death denied. The American revolution against limits eventually turns against the final, existential limitations: aging and death.

When elders are diminished, children suffer. Even under the most favoring conditions, good-enough childrearing requires major and continuing parental sacrifice. In the Druse case, the deprivations required by parenthood are not experienced as such: they are meaning-rich and accepted without complaint as part of the honored parental estate. Thus, Druse fathers often rebaptize themselves, taking on the name of their first-born son. Not surprisingly, Druse children and adolescents are among the sturdiest—psychologically as well as physically— that I have ever encountered.

But in America, fathers and mothers are increasingly hard put to find an unquestioned moral meaning in their parental obligations: Are they doing God's work or are they losers who have spun out of the fast track? The unremitting demands of children too often come into direct conflict with the adult's sense of entitlement, and parental requirements are increasingly given priority. The care of children is increasingly turned over to strangers in day-care centers. Divorce routinely is the path chosen to resolve parental disharmony, leaving children to be reared by the comparative strangers who become the parents' new mates. Ours is a society that too little honors and imbues with meaning the routine sacrifice and even heroism of parents and grandparents.

In sum, we have largely done away with our own Aqil, our own moral gerontocracy, only to find that we have put childhood at risk and are haunted by the terror of aging within ourselves. Our task is to create, in the framework of secular democracy, sources of meaning of the sort that are the birthright of semiliterate Druse.

REFERENCES

Cumming, E., & Henry, W. E. (1961). *Growing old: The process of disengagement.* New York: Basic Books.

Gutmann, D. (1973). The subjective politics of power: The dilemma of Post-Superego Man. *Social Research, 40,* 570–616.

Gutmann, D. (1994). *Reclaimed powers: Men and women in later life* (2nd ed.). Evanston, IL: Northwestern University Press.

Gutmann, D. (1997; orig. published 1974). Alternatives to disengagement: The old men of the Highland Druse. In D. Gutmann (Ed.), *The human elder in nature, culture and society.* Boulder, CO: Westview Press.

Riesman, D. (1969). *The lonely crowd* (2nd ed.). New Haven: Yale University Press.

Simmons, L. W. (1945). *The role of the aged in primitive society.* New Haven: Yale University Press.

SEVEN

Aging, Intimate Relationships, and Life Story among Gay Men

Bertram J. Cohler and Andrew J. Hostetler

EDITORS' INTRODUCTION This essay by Cohler and Hostetler is the first of three sets of case studies that show the way people's lives take shape and how their histories help decide what matters to them as they enter later life. In this essay and in the two autobiographical accounts that follow we can see how people express what they find important in life in the direction their lives take, even as their attention is absorbed by day-to-day challenges. They make known their values and goals not in declarations but in the relationships they establish, the decisions they make, and the lives they fashion.

Cohler and Hostettler show us two men now in the interval of the Third Age. Both are gay, reasonably affluent, and resident in a large city in the American Midwest. Each experienced the same cohort history: the same critical events that affected all those within their particular cohort. Each began adult life in a time when to be gay risked social exclusion except within a marginal and half-hidden gay community. Each has lived to see extraordinary change in social attitude; there is, if not complete social acceptance, at least wide support for acceptance.

Despite being of the same cohort, and having lived through the same history in the same region, the men presented by Cohler and Hostettler are different in the way they engage their social worlds. One is self-contained, unostentatious, conventional; the other is flamboyant, almost exhibitionist. The value they have placed on stability has been different. One has been, if not risk-averse, then at least uncomfortable with risk; the other has embraced it. The meanings they have given to relationships have been different. One has prized fidelity, while the other has searched for something else, perhaps the validity of the moment. Responsibility has mattered more to one of them, self-expression more to the other. As might be expected, the two men have had very different lives.

The authors accept, with Settersten (Chapter 4, this volume) that social and cultural processes shape later lives. They are alert to the special importance of cohort history. But Cohler and Hostetler also make us aware how much Third Age lives are extensions of an earlier life course. The way people understand themselves and their lives and the spheres of action available to them are largely decided by the choices and events of their earlier lives. Finally, Cohler and Hostetler remind us of the importance of the "scripts" that help us give meaning to the events of our lives. These scripts both help set our direction as we navigate among choices, and later help us make sense of the result.

The particular manner in which persons make meanings in the present regarding the course of their personal past may be most appropriately understood through study of the life story (Plath, 1980; Polkinghorne, 1988, 1996). Narratives of lived experience, or life stories, represent an effort to convince the listener or reader (including oneself as listener) of the coherence of a particular account of the past, both personal and collective (Mannheim, 1928; Plath, 1980; Polkinghorne, 1988, 1996). Through study of the life story, we can best understand how individuals create meaning out of personal experience and shared meanings. The significance of the narrated life story has been particularly well demonstrated in the collection edited by George Rosenwald and Richard Ochberg (1992), in Rubenstein's (1988) account of the process of collecting life stories from residents of a long-term care facility, in John Clausen's (1993) examination of the role of planful competence in the lives of men and women, and in Ruthellen Josselson's (1996) account of the lives through middle adulthood of a group of women who had been studied during their college years in the early seventies.

In this essay, we adopt a life-course framework for the developmental study of lesbian and gay lives, including the study of intimacy. This perspective starts from the assumption that individual development, from childhood to oldest age, is shaped by social, cultural, and historical processes, which are understood primarily through the concept of cohort (Elder, 1981, 1986, 1987, 1995). In addition to investigating cohort differences in the social organization of experience, the life-course perspective addresses shifts in shared, subjective meanings of experience, as reflected in the individual life story.

Parameters of the life story change, over both historical time and the course of particular lives, as a consequence of social and historical change. The life stories of gay men today show significant changes from those of the gay men of the last century, as a consequence of changed social and historical circumstances (Chauncey, 1994; Porter & Weeks, 1991).

The present generation of gay elders includes many men and women for whom the social changes of the tumultuous decade of the mid-1960s to mid-1970s had little relevance. Born between the First and Second World Wars, this generation was entering middle age at the time of the June 1969 riots at New York's Stonewall Inn. The news of these riots heralded the emergence of gay liberation on the model of the civil rights struggle of the preceding decade (Duberman, 1993; Young, 1995). This cohort of gay elders also includes some whose lives were very much affected by these developments, as well as a few who were active in promoting them. Life-story accounts provide an important means for understanding how different members of the same cohort may have been differently affected by events that all experienced at the same time in their lives and how these events now have different meaning for them.

The Context of the Present Study

We are now engaged in a continuing study of older gay and lesbian lives. Participants were recruited from a number of voluntary associations within the gay community following a presentation by our largely gay and lesbian research staff regarding the importance of understanding the interplay of sexual orientation, aging, and morale across the second half of life. From the outset, our work has been informed by recognition of the extent to which the research process is a reflexive activity involving both interviewer and participant (Myerhoff & Ruby, 1992; Watson & Weinberg, 1982). Life stories, such as those told by our study participants, are necessarily coconstructed by participant and interviewer (Cohler & Cole, 1996; Mishler, 1986; Weiss, 1994). We thought it important for virtually all our respondents to know that their interviewers were themselves gay or familiar with the issues of the gay community and could be relied on to be knowledgeable and sympathetic listeners.

Two life stories are discussed in this chapter. They are among the more than three dozen life stories we have been told in the course of studying gay and lesbian lives across the second half of life. These lives have been led in the context of what may be the most turbulent four decades of social change over the past century. We chose the two lives we discuss because they show how two men, members of the same cohort and similar in age and social background, can respond differently to the experiences of their cohort. Every life story can be understood only if there is awareness of its social and historical context (Clausen, 1993; Elder, 1981, 1995; Mannheim, 1928); on the other hand, lives of members of the same cohort can take different directions.

One man, Matthew, had a successful business career working for a prominent international business until forced to retire as a result of merger and downsizing. His career displayed the sequence and timing of increased responsibility and status that is expected in the lives of middle-class men in contemporary urban American society. Matthew realized this success while separating off his work from other aspects of his life. In particular, for more than three decades he kept secret from his work colleagues his relationship with his lover.

The other man, Jeffrey, led a much less conventional life. While on time for expectable career transitions, including gradual retirement in his late sixties, he made little effort to keep his gay sexual orientation secret from his work colleagues. He also participated actively in advancing causes important to the gay community. However, he has not been able to realize his hopes for a long-term partnership and continues to search for the elusive ideal companion.

Matthew: Making a Disciplined, Ordered, Successful Life

It is a peaceful, sunny weekday on Chicago's near North Side. The apartment buildings in the neighborhood were constructed in the 1960s in an effort to reclaim urban blight and now have become part of a vital and prosperous community a few blocks west of Lake Michigan. Matthew enjoys these quiet late spring days. Often he arises well after his lover of more than three decades has gone off to work. The victim of corporate mergers and downsizing a decade ago, Matthew has been able to live a comfortable and well-ordered life, supported by his retirement income and some family resources.

We first met Matthew while speaking about the psychological issues posed by being gay and gray at a group of gay business and professional men who meet monthly to network and to share their lives within the gay community. Altogether pleasant and at ease with his current life, he is active in the community as a volunteer. His life, as he describes it, has been fairly characteristic of his cohort of now older gay men who grew up in the shadows of the Second World War, were drafted and served overseas, and returned to civilian life in the economic boom years that followed the war's end.

Matthew comes from an old-line southern family of English descent on both sides. His family arrived in America well before the Revolutionary War. His father, a military officer, enjoyed a successful career, while his mother taught in a university. Both of his parents and his older brother lived well into later life. His recollection is that of a very loving, supportive, and caring family. His older brother was also career army, what Matthew describes as an "Ollie North" type. The family moved around a good deal during his youth, as families of career officers typically did, but these moves were expectable and did not disrupt the family. Ultimately, his father was transferred to the Pentagon, and the family settled in suburban Virginia.

Matthew was expected to make the army his career. He attended a prestigious military academy and was drafted into service following the bombing of Pearl Harbor. As was true for many men of his generation (Elder, 1986, 1987; Elder, Shanahan, & Clipp, 1994), the years of military service were personally satisfying for him. He had significant responsibilities for sensitive activities and found his work rewarding; it was not life-threatening.

Following the war, Matthew returned to college. He ultimately secured an MBA from one of the nation's most prestigious business schools. With an outstanding academic record, he had little difficulty obtaining an executive position. During his years of early adulthood, Matthew concentrated on his career and his relationships with a group of other men with whom he shared a large house in a Midwestern city. He reports that sex was not a big deal. He went out with women but never thought about his lack of sexual interest in them. His relationship with his family remained important, but his political beliefs were to the left of those of his militaristic father and brother, who were working actively on the campaign of George Wallace for president. He avoided political discussions at family reunions. Too busy with his career to think about personal or family tensions, he remained in contact but rather removed.

Matthew believes that any awareness within his Fortune 500 company of his sexual orientation would have finished his career. He believes that the other executives there would never have accepted an executive who was gay (his preferred term for his sexual orientation). To this day, his former business associates have no knowledge of his sexual orientation. He does sometimes wonder what sense they make of his never having married, but he thinks this was a minor concern to them, given his record of success at work. Although he has debated the wisdom of having kept his sexual orientation and his partnership a secret, he seriously doubts that business success could ever be compatible with alternative sexualities. He observes: "I wonder now . . . whether anyone going to business school, could anticipate building a career in a public, corporate or publicly held corporation if they were actively gay. I have no reason to believe that corporate culture as such, could accept that. . . . I think it would be very difficult, if not impossible."

Even when his gay friends tell him about organizations of gay and lesbian employees in their Fortune 500 companies, Matthew refuses to believe that going public about one's sexual orientation is compatible with career success. He continues to believe in not acknowledging his sexuality to anyone other than friends in the gay community. He readily admits that this concern makes it difficult for him to be the mentor to younger gay executives he thinks an older gay man should be.

Matthew recognizes that an older man who has never been married is often assumed to be gay. However, he maintains that it is up to others to reach that conclusion themselves. For example, Matthew recounts that the previous summer he had returned home and had met for lunch a woman who was in his high school class. When she asked him why had never married, he muttered something about believing that he would never have been a good father. He says that occasionally people ask him if he is gay but that he turns the question aside.

Matthew has adopted the dominant sexual script or master narrative of the gay community regarding his sexual orientation (Plummer, 1995; Simon & Gagnon, 1984, 1988). He believes that homosexuality is inherited and that psychological and family factors play little role in determining sexual orientation. He recalls that as a child he enjoyed playing with dolls but was discouraged from such activity when he was six by a nursemaid, on orders from his mother. Beyond that, Matthew reports little awareness of his sexuality until his late thirties, when he happened to walk into a gay bar. He thinks now he must have known about his sexuality, but there was little public discussion of homosexuality and he certainly had no word to attach to his wishes. At the same time, Matthew notes that he is not the stereotyped gay man and reports few feelings of guilt or self-criticism attached to being gay. He has few regrets about the manner in which he has led his life or about his decision to remain secretive about his sexuality at work and in the larger community.

Matthew met his longtime lover (his term for their relationship) at a party. This happened at about the time that he was first able to find words for his sexuality. It was pretty much love at first sight: Matthew and his lover, who is a few years the younger, moved in together and have been together since. Matthew said that his lover, an accountant with a major firm, also believed in being secretive at work about their relationship. His lover has at times had difficulty with alcohol.

The couple's social life is largely confined to dinner parties with other gay couples. Matthew reports that recently, while his lover was out of town on business, he was invited to a dinner party where there were mainly older single gay men. He reports that he found the discussion, centering on complaints about being single and on elaborate sexual fantasies, to be distasteful. He says:

> I have never been as bored in my life. . . . All they wanted to talk about was their health problems or their sexual fantasies. . . . The reason we enjoy the gay couples' groups that we have had was because we have the normal, straight dinner party, where people talked about politics, music, you name it, but nothing gay . . . because most gay couples are not obsessed.

Matthew notes that just like straight people, gay people worry about getting older without having anyone to care for them. He is concerned about his own aging. He was recently found to have prostate cancer, for which he has been taking radiation treatments. While his illness has not interfered with his life, it has given him some pause regarding the problems of being older and without support. At the same time, in his usual stoic manner, he reports that will not let himself physically deteriorate and that he has prepared a living will, which he has shared with his lover.

Matthew is clearly satisfied with his present life in retirement. He does note that retirement was initially somewhat stressful and that he sought the advice of a psychiatrist in making this transition. He is now comfortable with it. His prostate cancer has not had an adverse impact on his morale.

Matthew is passionate about "contract bridge"; indeed, this is one of the few areas of his life where he shows any passion at all. Twice a week he plays bridge at a local gay-owned restaurant and, predictably, he maintains that the fact that the restaurant is a focus for gay community activities is largely irrelevant. He recently won an award as "volunteer of the year" for counseling gay men regarding their finances and lifestyle. Although committed to this volunteer work, Matthew says that he does it because it is something he can do, not because he is gay.

In his seventies, Matthew is a man who has through his life displayed strong-as-steel self-control. He has given himself little opportunity to acknowledge areas in his life where he might have had concerns. Nor has he spent much time thinking about his sexual life. He believes that being gay is less an important part of his life than having been successful at work and having made his way in the world.

As we have found in talking with other men of this generation who remained secretive about their sexuality at work, Matthew never faced the overt discrimination experienced by the now middle-aged cohort who publicly acknowledged their sexual lifeway in the aftermath of Stonewall and Gay Liberation and demanded respect at work and in the community (Herdt, 1997; Hostetler & Herdt, 1998; Ridge, Minichiello, & Plummer, 1997). In the same way, as is characteristic for his cohort, Matthew has had few friends who have had AIDS; he has been relatively shielded from the epidemic.

Matthew does not view his relationship with his lover as a marriage, nor does he use any other term that might be used by a heterosexual couple to describe a long-term relationship. While he is somewhat reluctant to talk about the relationship, it appears to add a sense of order or balance to his life. Yet he displays little of what might be considered love. It seems likely that, even if he were straight, Matthew would have sought a life partnership more out of the recognition that such a partnership was a necessary and expectable arrangement than as a result of love or passion. He has made little room in his life for passion.

Overall, Matthew believes that the larger society demands that he meet its expectations of the life course of middle-class heterosexual men. He has done his best to comply (Herdt, 1997; Hostetler & Herdt, 1998). At the same time, he is bemused with the career success of gay friends in subsequent age cohorts who appear to have successfully integrated their personal and their work lives. These friends, he recognizes, do not share his belief that penalties must accompany acknowledgment of a gay lifeway.

Jeffrey: Struggling to Complete a Biography of Desire

The apartment on the top floor of a three-story walk-up, in a neighborhood noted for its concentration of gay men (about a third of the residents), is cluttered with antiques, a variety of art projects of mixed media in a half-finished state, books and magazines, and a number of packing boxes. The visitor has to step carefully in order not to bump into furniture and boxes. Jeffrey apologizes for the clutter, explaining that his lover of the past few years has decided to take a separate apartment on the floor below and is in the process of moving his belongings. Jeffrey has been through this before, and it doesn't seem to faze him. He explains that his lover, one of many Asian-American men in his life, is an academic who needs more privacy for his writing.

Jeffrey at age 71 has recently retired from the large advertising firm, of which he had been a founding member and the director of creative services. Affluent, with a significant pension, Jeffrey has both the time and money for the extensive travel he so much enjoys. Just as was the case for Matthew, Jeffrey was in his early adulthood little aware of the sexual lifeway that has characterized the second half of his life. Married young, Jeffrey first became aware of what he describes as "bisexual tendencies" in his forties. He traces his awareness to a book he picked up in an airport book shop while on one of his frequent trips to New York. The main character in the book was struggling with his own sexuality and going to the gay bath houses.

Jeffrey all of a sudden recognized the struggle of the book's protagonist as similar to his own increasing feelings of restlessness and his increasing dissatisfaction with the infrequent sexual relations in his own marriage. Upon his arrival in New York he looked up bath houses in the Yellow Pages, found a listing for the St. Mark's Baths, which he knew from reading the novel must be gay, and participated in reciprocal oral sex that very night. He says, "It was . . . like somebody turned on a switch. That was my first experience and that was when I sort of came out. . . . I mean I knew what I was doing and really enjoyed it." Jeffrey says that this experience convinced him that he was bisexual and perhaps even gay.

Over the course of the next ten years, Jeffrey struggled with life in both worlds. His frequent travels made it possible for him to have sexual experiences in a chain of gay bath houses around the country. He also participated in several same-gender sexual affairs of varying length and intensity, including intimate contacts with one of his daughter's boyfriends and a long-term off-and-on affair with his son's former roommate. Jeffrey has never experienced closure of this relationship; it ended with the younger partner drifting to other relationships, only to return once more and then again depart.

Finally, as he approached 50, Jeffrey decided that leading a double life was too complex. He proposed to his wife that they get divorced. His wife insisted that they first try counseling. The couple attended several sessions, and then Jeffrey went alone. Finally, the psychiatrist met with the couple and told them that there was little hope for their relationship. Jeffrey was clearly gay, and his wife couldn't accept his being both gay and married. The couple decided to divorce.

Jeffrey found a room in a transient hotel near the gay community. He describes this as the worst period of his life. He found his quarters depressing and his life barren of social contacts. He says his former wife was very supportive during this period and that his children tried to help as best they could. However, both his daughter and his son had lives to lead as adults, and his wife had returned to work on a full-time basis. During this time Jeffrey found his creativity at a low ebb. He struggled to make a new life for himself, with occasional bouts of depression, drinking, and forays to the bath houses.

Jeffrey's coming out occurred just after the height of the sexual revolution. Popular culture, such as the musical show *Hair*, had increased awareness regarding the possibilities of different lifestyles. Many of Jeffrey's younger colleagues in the creative department of his firm had endorsed the sexual revolution and were accepting of his sexual struggles. One of these colleagues, also gay, told Jeffrey about a church with a largely gay congregation and offered to go with him to services. Immersion in the life of the church, about six months after being on his own, led to Jeffrey's first active involvement in the gay community.

Jeffrey was drawn to the gay minister of the church, a middle-aged man who had also been married and had young adult offspring. While their relationship was short-lived, it did lead to Jeffrey's increased involvement in the church and the gay community. Subsequently, Jeffrey was able to employ his considerable creative talents to help other institutions in the gay community develop effective advertising for fundraising events. Jeffrey's efforts were appreciated by others in the gay community, and he was given considerable recognition for them.

The second-born of a fraternal twin pair, Jeffrey is at a loss to explain the emergence of a gay sexual lifeway at midlife. He notes that his twin brother is married, has had children, and apparently has little interest in same-gender sexuality. Still, he believes that his adoption of a gay sexual lifeway probably reflects a genetic determinant of homosexuality. Certainly, there was little in his past that could have predicted his decision at midlife to become gay.

Jeffrey's twin brother was a good athlete, was president of his high school class, and resembled his bold, tall, handsome, athletic father, who traced his Swedish ancestry back to the Vikings. Jeffrey remembers having tried at first to compete with his brother. He gave up when his brother began excelling in all sports. Jeffrey particularly remembers the feeling of being left out when his older brother, his twin brother, and his father used to rent a plane to go fishing in a remote part of the Canadian wilderness. Somehow he never got invited on these trips. He believes that his family thought he wouldn't enjoy the wilderness trip. Still, he observes, being excluded from family athletic and outdoors endeavors contributed to his feeling that he wasn't like the rest of his family. Later, both his brothers went into the business started by his father. He continued to feel apart from the interests of the other men in his family.

Consistent with the present dominant narrative for gay men (Plummer, 1995; Savin-Williams, 1997; Simon & Gagnon, 1984, 1988), Jeffrey recalls as a child having felt different from other boys his age. Most of his classmates were interested in sports, girls, and cars. He was an oddball who took art courses. His parents, in an effort to help him with what they saw as shyness, enrolled him in Boy Scouts, where he ultimately became an Eagle Scout. Looking back on his high school days, Jeffrey believes that this experience in scouting, where he excelled, provided the necessary self-esteem to improve his relationships at high school. He became more popular, had a girlfriend, and enjoyed the admiration of his friends for his success at school. At the same time, Jeffrey still felt that he was different from his peers.

A somewhat older boy who lived down the block, who subsequently married and moved away but is still in touch with Jeffrey, took an interest in Jeffrey and invited him over. The conversation got around to sex, and the two began hesitant sexual exploration. Over time some closeness developed between the two boys. Following high school Jeffrey won an art scholarship and lived in the local YMCA, where another boy living on the floor invited him to his room and to what ended up as an intense sexual experience. Jeffrey reports that he never connected same-gender sexual experiences with other men during his youth with the possibility that he might be gay. Indeed, he says that he was a late-bloomer who was pretty naive about the world about him through much of his teen-age years.

With the war's end, following completion of college (he had been drafted late in the war but never shipped overseas), Jeffrey moved to Chicago to find a job. He had been told by friends that a girl he had known in high school had also moved to Chicago and was urged to look her up. Having recovered from his adolescent shyness, Jeffrey had dated during college. Jeffrey called up his hometown friend; they met, liked each other, and soon became engaged. He says that his hesitant sexual advances while dating were of the sort that characterized his friends during high school. He purchased a sex manual in order that he might learn about his wife's sexuality and what was expected of him sexually. His wife was the first woman with whom he had sex. His wife was also sexually inexperienced and even after their marriage didn't seem to really enjoy sexuality.

Asked about his decision to get married, Jeffrey observes: "A lot of my life has been the tension between other people's expectations and the cultural expectations that are around me and my own possibilities and choices. . . . That's the reason I got married." Aware of his cohort's norms for the sequence and timing of life-course events, Jeffrey complied. Without any sense of strain or hesitancy, yet also without a strong sense of conviction, he was swept along by an understanding of the life course he shared with a generation determined to make up for lost time to the war.

Considering other narratives of the lives of successful middle-class men (Levinson, 1978; Sheehy, 1976), it is tempting to claim that Jeffrey encountered a midlife crisis that led to his decision to explore same-gender sexuality. While not conceiving of it as a crisis, Jeffrey acknowledges that he had read Gail Sheehy's book. He believes that her discussion of expectable changes with the advent of midlife was one of several influences in his decision to seek a gay lifestyle with the advent of midlife.

As in other coming-out stories in our series, the popular discourse of a particular time played a significant role in Jeffrey's thinking about himself and his narrative account of his life. Here, as elsewhere, the continuing interplay of history and personal biography within and across cohorts in large measure shapes the story that cohort members tell of their lived experience. As with other members of his cohort, Jeffrey had new access to the words of others through novels and biographies in a way not possible in the time before Stonewall. He also had the social acknowledgment and increasing social visibility of alternative sexual expression brought about by expanded social awareness (D'Emilio & Freedman, 1997; Duberman, 1993; Young, 1995).

To a greater extent than the life story told by Matthew, Jeffrey's life story reflects the significant impact of the social changes of the time on his own sexual lifeway. Indeed, Jeffrey views these social changes, including their representation in popular culture, as central in defining his own sexuality and in reordering his account of his own biography.

Matthew's approach to living has emphasized discipline in both himself and others. This seems much less true for Jeffrey. Jeffrey continues to explore his sexuality in ways that would be unacceptable for Matthew. His retirement travel is most often to Southeast Asia, where he enjoys the company of younger men in brothels and escort services.

Presently, Jeffrey is ending an intense relationship with a younger Asian-American man, an instructor in an area college. He has been together with this younger man for nearly four years. Jeffrey met him at a local association devoted to American-Asian gay friendships. His friend was there with another older man whom he had met through a newspaper advertisement but was attracted to Jeffrey. Now, however, Jeffrey reports that he is seeking sensual rather than sexual satisfaction and that what he seeks is incompatible with living with someone else.

In his seventies, Jeffrey has had his share of disappointments, chief among which is that his son developed problems with alcohol abuse. This led eventually to family involvement with twelve-step programs. Further, his son is now divorced and shares custody of Jeffrey's two grandchildren with Jeffrey's former daughter-in-law. Jeffrey still does not understand the source of this marital breakup but guesses that it must have had something to do with his son's abuse of alcohol.

Nevertheless, Jeffrey reports that he is very happy with his life. He keeps in close touch with his former wife and two children. His frequent travels and their attendant sensual activities provide Jeffrey with an outlet for his sexuality. His many friends and intense involvement in the local gay community provide him with the same sense of personal fulfillment and accomplishment that had been provided by his work. These associations also keep him in touch with younger generations. Indeed, Jeffrey spends little time with men and women his own age. Not only does he seek out younger sexual partners but he also prefers younger men and women as friends. Active, vital, and committed, Jeffrey feels that over the course of middle and later life he has finally realized a life story in little need of further revision.

Conclusion

The life circumstances of Matthew and Jeffrey were in many ways the same: they were of nearly the same age and social position, were both retired, and both affluent. Both had publicly affirmed their same-gender sexual lifeway first at midlife. Yet they were markedly different in their ways of negotiating the course of gay middle and later adulthood.

For Matthew, who led a life conforming to that expected by family and community, work and personal life were sharply divided. Nor has Matthew been especially active in the gay community. He and his lover confine their life to a small number of other gay couples with whom they have dinner and play bridge. His relationship with his lover reflects the larger society's expectations of an enduring intimate relationship. Jeffrey made his personal life known at his work, became highly active in the gay community, and never established a long-term relationship.

At least a part of the difference between the lives of the two men may be accounted for by their different work situations.

As Matthew views corporate life, public acknowledgment of same-gender sexuality, although increasingly possible, would represent an intangible barrier to further career advancement. Jeffrey, responsible for creative artistic achievement as well as management of his small firm, saw fewer constraints. Indeed, he enjoyed being able to have as colleagues other men who acknowledged a same-gender sexuality. In his work situation, more than was true in Matthew's, the only fact that mattered was creative response to a client's needs.

Many of the adults in this oldest cohort report a sexual script or dominant narrative reflecting the presumption that sexual orientation was a fixed and essential characteristic (Plummer, 1995; Savin-Williams, 1997; Simon & Gagnon, 1984, 1988). They believe themselves always to have been gay (Schafer, 1995; Settersten & Hägestad, 1996; Settersten & Mayer, 1997). Linked with this appear to be at least two predominant sexual lifeways, varying by whether self-definition as gay came early or late.

One group of older gay men and women is characterized as becoming aware of same-gender sexual wishes during childhood or adolescence. Typically, they led a quiet life, often with partners, very much in the model of heterosexual counterparts. These men and women distinguished between their public and private life; they did not believe that their sexual orientation was relevant to any aspect of their life at work or in the community. Matthew's life story is characteristic of this group.

A second group of men and women first discovered their gay sexuality during the two decades of change in society's understanding of sexual orientation. Men and women in this second group had often not been aware of same-gender sexual desire until particular life circumstances, within a time of increased visibility of alternative sexualities, facilitated such awareness (Herdt, 1997; Hostetler & Herdt, 1998; Ridge, Minichiello, & Plummer, 1997). Our larger study of gay and lesbian sexuality across the second half of life includes many men and women whose stories are similar to that of Jeffrey. Most often married, with adolescent or adult offspring, these men and women happened to meet another man or woman with whom they first experienced same-gender sexual desire. Either this first relationship, or a subsequent one, led them to divorce and to begin a long-term relationship with their newly found partner.

While there seems to be a master or dominant narrative "explaining" sexual orientation for a cohort (Plummer, 1995), there may also be significant intracohort variation associated with these alternative sexual pathways or lifeways across the adult life course. For example, one recently retired man participating in a focus group in our larger study reported that he met his life partner in late middle age at a time when his wife was often out of town on business. Invited out by a gay coworker to a gay bar popular among middle-aged and older gay men, this man met another man with whom he fell in love. He divorced his professionally successful and preoccupied wife and has now lived with this man for more than a decade.

Study of lived experience across generations must be informed by the social and historical changes characteristic of particular cohorts. As Elder (1981, 1995) has shown, recognition of the impact of social and historical change on narratives of lived experience leads to a more complex and textured understanding of the course of life than has been realized in much traditional study of life transitions.

NOTE

The interviews on which this chapter is based were part of a larger study of life course and provision of mental health services by the Evelyn Hooker Center for Gay and Lesbian Mental Health of the University of Chicago and Horizons Community

Services Center. Nearly fifty older gay men and women, recruited from gay community political and social groups, were interviewed for the study. This chapter is dedicated to the memory of Keith Ocheltree, a participant in our study who died of a long illness as this chapter was being written.

REFERENCES

Chauncey, G., Jr. (1994). *Gay New York: Gender, urban culture and the making of the gay male world, 1890–1940.* New York: HarperCollins.

Clausen, J. (1993). *American lives: Looking back at the children of the Great Depression.* New York: Free Press.

Cohler, B. J., & Cole, T. R. (1996). Studying older lives: Reciprocal acts of telling and listening. In J. E. Birren, G. M. Kenyon, J.-E. Ruth, J. J. F Schroots, & T. Svensson (Eds.), *Aging and biography: Explorations in adult development* (pp. 61–76). New York: Springer.

D'Emilio, J., & Freedman, E. B. (1997). *Intimate matters: A history of sexuality in America* (2nd ed.). Chicago: University of Chicago Press.

Duberman, M. (1993). *Stonewall.* New York: St. Martin's Press.

Elder, G. H., Jr. (1981). Social history and life experience. In D. H. Eichorn, J. A. Clausen, N. Hann, M. P. Honzik, & P. H. Mussen (Eds.), *Present and past in middle life* (pp. 3–32). San Diego: Academic Press.

Elder, G. H., Jr. (1986). Military times and turning points in men's lives. *Developmental Psychology, 22,* 233–245.

Elder, G. H., Jr. (1987). War mobilization and the life course: A cohort of World War II veterans. *Sociological Focus, 2,* 449–472.

Elder, G. H., Jr. (1995). The life-course paradigm: Social change and individual development. In P. Moen, G. H. Elder, Jr., & K. Lüscher (Eds.), *Examining Lives in context: Perspectives on the ecology of human development* (pp. 101–139). Washington, DC: American Psychological Association.

Elder, G. H. Jr., Shanahan, M., & Clipp, E. (1994). When war comes to men's lives: Life course patterns in family, work, and health. *Psychology of Aging, 9,* 5–16.

Herdt, G. (1997). *Same sex, different cultures.* Boulder, CO: Westview Press.

Herdt, G., Beeler, J., & Rawls, T. (1997). Life course diversity among older lesbians and gay men: A study in Chicago. *Journal of Gay, Lesbian and Bisexual Identity, 2,* 231–246.

Hostetler, A., & Herdt, G. (1998). Culture, sexual lifeways and developmental subjectivities: Rethinking sexual taxonomies. *Social Research, 65,* 249–290.

Josselson, R. (1996). *Revising herself: The story of women's identity from college to midlife.* New York: Oxford University Press.

Levinson, D. (1978). *The seasons of a man's life.* New York: Knopf.

Mannheim, K. (1928). The problem of generations. In K. Mannheim, *Essays on the sociology of knowledge* (pp. 276–322). London: Routledge & Kegan Paul.

Mishler, E. (1986). *Research interviewing: Context and narrative.* Cambridge: Harvard University Press.

Myerhoff, B., & Ruby, J. (1992). A crack in the mirror: Reflective perspectives in anthropology. In M. Kaminsky (Ed.), *Remembered lives: The work of ritual, storytelling and growing older* (pp. 307–340). Ann Arbor: University of Michigan Press.

Plath, D. (1980). Contours of consociation: Lessons from a Japanese narrative. In P. B. Baltes & O. G. Brim, Jr. (Eds.), *Lifespan development and behavior* (Vol. 3, pp. 287–305). New York: Academic Press.

Plummer, K. (1995). *Telling sexual stories: Power, change and social worlds.* London: Routledge.

Polkinghorne, D. E. (1988). *Narrative knowing and the human sciences.* Albany: State University of New York Press.

Polkinghorne, D. E. (1996). Narrative knowing and the study of lives. In J. E. Birren, G. M. Kenyon, J.-E. Ruth, J. J. F. Schroots, & T. Svensson (Eds.), *Aging and biography: Explorations in adult development* (pp. 61–76). New York: Springer.

Porter, K., & Weeks, J. (1991). *Between the acts: Lives of homosexual men, 1885–1967*. London: Routledge.

Ridge, D., Minichiello, V., & Plummer, D. (1997). Queer connections: Community, "the scene" and an epidemic. *Journal of Contemporary Ethnography, 26,* 146–181.

Rosenwald, G. C., & Ochberg, R. L. (Eds.). (1992). *Storied Lives: The cultural politics of self-understanding.* New Haven: Yale University Press.

Rubenstein, R. (1988). Stories told: In-depth interviewing and the structure of its insights. In S. Reinharz & G. D. Rowles (Eds.), *Qualitative gerontology* (pp. 128–146). New York: Springer.

Savin-Williams, R. (1997). . . . *And then I became gay: Young men's stories.* New York: Routledge.

Schafer, R. (1995). The evolution of my views on nonnormative sexual practices. In T. Domenici & R. C. Lesser (Eds.), *Disorienting sexuality: Psychoanalytic reappraisals of sexual identities* (pp. 187–202). New York: Routledge.

Settersten, R. A., Jr., & Hägestad, G. (1996). What's the latest? Cultural age deadlines for family transitions. *Gerontologist, 36,* 178–188.

Settersten, R. A., Jr., & Mayer, K. U. (1997). The measurement of age, age structuring, and the life-course. *Annual Review of Sociology, 23,* 233–261.

Sheehy, G. (1976). Passages: Predictable crises of adult life. New York: Dutton.

Simon, W., & Gagnon, J. H. (1984). Sexual scripts. *Transaction, 22,* 53–60.

Simon, W., & Gagnon, J. H. (1988). A sexual scripts approach. In J. Geer & W.T. O'Donohue (Eds.), *Theories of human sexuality* (pp. 363–383). New York: Plenum.

Watson, D. R., & Weinberg, T. S. (1982). Interviews and the interactional construction of accounts of homosexual identity. *Social Analysis 11*, 56–78.

Weiss, R. (1994). *Learning from strangers: The art and method of qualitative interview studies.* New York: Free Press.

Young, I. (1995). *The Stonewall experiment: A gay psychohistory.* London: Cassell.

EIGHT

Looking for Meaning in a Life's Experience

Robert Morris

EDITORS' INTRODUCTION   When we asked Bob
Morris to provide this chapter, he was in his late eighties.
Although still vigorous, and still contributing to the field of
social policy, he was at the farther edge of the Third Age.

As we write this introduction, it has been three years
since Bob submitted it and four years since we asked
him to write it. His life has been affected by loss and by
the inroads of time. He is in the midst of passage from
the Third Age. Nevertheless he pursues his work on the
meaning of aging and the societal response to the aging
demographics.

Two years after he submitted this chapter, Bob sustained the severe blow of his wife's death. In the chapter,
Bob talks about Sara's need for him: he cooked her
meals, helped her dress, helped her in and out of her
wheelchair. She needed his help ever more often. Bob
found that his wife's need for him and his love for her
gave him an ongoing sense of purpose.

When his wife died Bob lost the person who had been
his companion for fifty-nine years. Despite his grief, Bob
kept on meeting with his colleagues, and he maintained
his active and productive professional life. He regularly
traveled between Baltimore, where he lived, and Boston,
where he had university affiliations.

By the end of the year after his wife's death, at age 89, Bob thought it prudent to prepare for a future in which his mobility might be impaired. He was in good health, but he had neither children nor nearby family. He found a small continuing-care community in Baltimore that would provide him with independent living space for home, office, and entertaining and that had supportive services available should they be needed. He established a program in Sara's memory at Brandeis University through a charitable annuity trust, provided modestly in his will for two greatnieces, and moved in.

Only a few months after the move, Bob fell in his apartment. The fall did not give rise to serious health problems but did leave him with minor problems affecting his balance. He now uses a cane when walking on uneven terrain. Nevertheless, he still contributes to the field of social welfare studies as a consultant, editor, and mentor. He is also an adviser to a multicity demonstration program in the area of long-term care. The supportive services of his new community make all this easier to do.

When we asked Bob to write an autobiographical chapter, we anticipated that he would show us how a steady commitment to idealistic goals provides continuity to life well into the Third Age. He has indeed done that. But he has also shown us that there is an inevitable transition from the Third Age even for someone as energetic and engaged as he. At some point physical frailty limits mobility. Sustaining relationships may be lost; the circle of family and friends from whom life's meaning is drawn may narrow. And yet, as Bob demonstrates in his own life, it remains possible to continue to be engaged by lifelong concerns, to find new intellectual challenges, and to continue to contribute to one's community.

What changes as we grow older? And, among all the things that might change, which must we adapt to, and which can we slow, if not avoid? Is it inescapable that our senses lose acuity, our capacities for work diminish, our energies be depleted? And are there guides for how to behave or act when sad times appear? Should we anticipate decline by moving, while it is still easy for us to move, to retirement villages or condominiums that provide assisted living facilities? Or should we ignore aging and, to the extent that we can, live for the day? This last is an approach to life perhaps more easily achieved by the very young, for whom a day can stretch endlessly, but it may nevertheless appeal to those of us for whom this day appears likely to be better than the next, and the next better than the one that follows.

One approach is to stave off the time when these issues must be considered. And, in truth, much effort now goes into preventing or avoiding not only illness but growing old. Men and women no longer young but not yet old add vitamins to their diets, reduce their intake of fats, patronize health clubs, and read texts on healthful living.

Whole industries have arisen to serve middle-aged as well as young adults who wish to maintain their vitality as far into the future as possible. Recent decades have seen a flood of writing and reporting on how to age better, in which a variety of adjectives—successful, healthy, satisfying, productive—are used to modify and detoxify "aging" and to counter the image of later life as a time of feebleness, loss of function, and dependency. The movement began decades ago when it became popular to argue that life begins at forty rather than ending about then, as was true of the average life span at the turn of the century. The changes in average life span since that time can be seen as nothing short of miraculous, but equally impressive is the reduced morbidity of those in their later years. The extension of life has been achieved not by reducing the mortality of the ill but rather by extending the years of wellness. A recent book by two eminent gerontologists, John Rowe and

Robert Kahn, suggests that late-life wellness is a reasonable goal entirely achievable by many, if not by most.

In response to these developments, businesses have arisen to furnish people in their later years with new experiences, new leisure activities, and new ways to be usefully occupied. The arts and crafts of the senior center have been augmented by university courses often available without cost to seniors. Travel opportunities are provided not only by companies and agents who deal with everyone in the population but also by specialists, such as Elderhostel, that target their programs to the retired. There has been renewed academic and public interest in the ways elders can contribute to their children's families and to the functioning of their communities and churches. Indeed, utilizing the elderly volunteer is sometimes seen as a reasonable alternative to relying on government-funded service providers.

Simon Patten, an early social economist, recognized in 1880 that a time would come when technology and science would create a surplus of workers and so make early retirement, along with later entrance into the labor force, an attractive social option. The alternative, he said, would be widespread unemployment or underemployment. Patten envisioned older retired workers using their energies to invigorate civic life. Perhaps some of this is happening; some older people do act as aides in schools and hospitals, though probably not very many. But for the most part, it would seem, people's use of time in their later lives is very much like their use of time in their earlier lives, and if they did not volunteer much in their thirties and forties and fifties—and most did not—they do not volunteer much in their sixties and seventies. Instead, those whose earlier leisure was spent with family spend the increased leisure of later life with family, and those who were work-centered continue to be, though at a reduced level. And perhaps this is good enough.

Some Personal Testimony

I am in later life myself now—in my eighties—and I have lived through the changes I describe here. They seem, actually, less vivid than the great events of our time: depression and war and the postwar expansion. I think I have been like others, doing the best I could with the givens of my lifetime, probably not thinking much about life's meaning, trying instead to act in response to the challenges and opportunities that events have provided. I have tried to act in conformity with my beliefs and values, which for me, as for others, have been to be responsible and loving to others in my family and to do well enough in my work to maintain my self-respect.

To be more specific, my life course now seems to me to have been neither planned nor, as far as I can see, foreordained. Instead it seems to have been a consequence of choices between alternative paths made on the basis of values and short-term goals of which, often, I was not clearly aware. There was, in addition, a certain amount of pure drift. Somehow—I cannot be sure exactly how—it has added up to a gratifying and, I hope, useful career. I have been able to continue even after formal retirement.

My parents were poor in the 1930s, as were most Americans, but we did not consider ourselves poverty-stricken. Neither parent was religious, but both kept tenuous links to their ethnic origins. My parents divorced early, and from then on my mother worked hard at the low pay then available. I also worked, selling newspapers, and in addition we had the help of a more comfortable aunt and grandparents. Life was the sum of what one did to survive.

A municipal university made higher education possible, provided I worked at the same time. There, I joined with a few schoolmates to form a tiny group interested in literature and music and the ideas about society afloat at the time, much of them with echoes from a romantic nineteenth-century tradition. From that time forward, an important activity for me has been discussion of ideas and writings in which can be found the descriptions of human condition in its many forms.

In college I mixed sociology and economics with musical and literary and theatrical interests without much sense of direction. Faculty advisors questioned my apparently aimless course of study but nevertheless tolerated it. After graduation I first tried law school, with the help of the beneficent aunt, and then social work, not from any conviction about a career in social work but because there were jobs to be had. In the 1930s a course of social work study brought with it an agency job with a minuscule stipend (I recall it as less than $50 a month). That was salary enough to support both myself and my mother. I had told my school of social work that I was interested in research into the causes of social distress, and so they had placed me in the Federal Emergency Relief Administration. Ironically, my social work training had mainly been in individual case work, for which the relief agency had no real place. Probably the experience increased my skepticism about formulae to solve human problems. It did not, however, make me cynical. I still believed—and have continued to believe—in the value of organized response to human problems.

I drifted into other casework agency positions for a few years until World War II provided an opportunity to link the needs of a working class to the social welfare institutions. Having been attracted to the new white-collar trade union movement, I was fortunate to be given the opportunity to create an agency to link the trade unions and the welfare establishment. Previously these two institutions had had little to do with each other, with suspicions about radicalism on the one side and disdain for reaction on the other. I was drafted from that into the army, where I served as a conscientious objector with no organized religious base for the stance, only a private conviction derived from where I knew not.

After the war, and some initial floundering, I ended up as a social planning consultant with a national agency that served a network of urban institutions. There I began to grapple with ideas about how social institutions resist change but could nevertheless be gotten to change in response to new needs and new conditions. I recognized that change is often a difficult and risky task, but I thought that it might be possible to find principles or approaches that could prove useful.

The GI Bill of Rights enabled me to return to school for a doctorate, and I ended up at a university that was launching a new doctoral program. The program—the first I believe of its kind—provided a course of studies in social welfare. I gave my attention to the impact of government policies and decisions on individual well-being, as well as on social work as a field and on its private agencies.

I found myself writing about theories of change and their application in several areas—family services, child welfare, urban planning among them. I accidentally met a leader in the then new field of social gerontology and now shifted my attention to the concerns and possibilities there. None of this can be said to have been part of any conscious attention to the larger meanings of my activities or to the question of what I was doing with my life. But in retrospect I can see that my intellectual interests had always been broad rather than technically narrow and had always ranged over a number of areas, from public affairs to economics, to social theories, to literature, and to the actions of social institutions.

Albeit not consciously, I had developed a questioning sense, a skepticism about life's events, although without becoming cynical. Perhaps this outlook was heightened by my reading, which was usually broad, ranging from drama to nineteenth-century English novels to poetry to a little politics. I have always been curious, and I have always wanted to do and say something about the contradictions I encountered everywhere between expressed aims and actual behaviors.

From all the foregoing, a career resulted, with some success. It was hardly a designed or purposeful one. Underlying it, perhaps, was curiosity about human institutions and concern about their effects on human beings.

In the course of this, I remained a deist, in the sense that I believe that there is some pattern to the world but not one designed by a knowable, human-focused deity. If there is such, science cannot comprehend it; this is the realm of faith. If there is not, and yet there is a pattern of some kind, we cannot find its purposes—its "meaning"—but we can try to understand how it works. Here is the domain of science.

If there has been continuity in all this, it probably consists of this: that I have been unable to predict ahead of time what opportunities might arise to support myself, while acting on a somewhat vague sense of responsibility for others. I think my notions of "doing good" and "helping others" derive from my childhood experiences. My understanding of what they entail has changed over the years and continues to change. I believe that the lives of most people are lived not too differently.

Looking around Me Today

The society we live in today is different in many ways from the one in which I grew up. In a pragmatic and scientific era people have had to adapt to major change in family life, in the nature of interpersonal relationships, in the nature of community. Ideas of individual growth and experience become individual rights as powerful as family rights. Marriage is not seen as necessarily lifelong. Community is no longer defined by living together in close-knit clans. Instead ideas of freedom and individual liberties have created extended communities where some members stay where they were born and their children can move away, far or near. Urban life permits some clustering of affinity groups in neighborhoods, but over time these too sprawl away to other and new locations.

My favored suggestion about the procession through life is the maturing awareness of how our personal need for others and others' need for us change with the years. Most of human organization and life itself is made up of interdependencies: from womb to birth to growing up, with its separation from parents, to creating new networks of friends or new families, to computer-age retirement while healthy, and finally to the time when our functional abilities fail.

Since the Greek philosophers we have recognized the reciprocal nature between giver and receiver in acts of charity and philanthropy. Today we accept that we need some collective provision to save us from illness and loss of income and loneliness for which we must contribute either through personal giving to others of time and energy or through the taxes that assure that some safety net is there for all. This does not solve all problems, but it is what we can do, alone and together.

This need for others has had increasing salience for me as I have aged. During thirty years of work as a gerontologist I acted on the collective provision dimension that was popular during the expansion of the welfare state. But as my wife's physical ills worsened I found that I had new reason for recognizing what one person can do for another, and I have witnessed my own love deepen and take on a wholly new form as my wife increasingly depended on me for physical and emotional help. My wife hated her dependency and yet was not able to escape it, though she minimized it as much as she could. On my part, I found that working to help this one person deepened my understanding of helping beyond what I had intellectually articulated during my career.

Still, having helpers of all kinds is useful, and recently more of my professional effort has gone to changing the system so that supplemental personal care can be more available at home. My efforts at system-changing continue work I have long been engaged in, but now I act with more personal understanding. Many families and lone individuals choose a nursing home or a life care community as a way to find the community and the support they need and cannot find with family or friends. For my wife, and for myself as well, having each other, some additional family members, and a satisfying friendship network was and has been, to this point, fully adequate.

I find that the human effort to deal with the reality of the body and mind limitations represents not only a significant entry into the end stages of life but a personally enriching and enlarging part of the life cycle. The reality of our frailties is knowable, and learning about that reality can be valuable. However, I believe that while much of the search for prevention and wellness is useful and a proper approach for a scientific and basically secular population, it does nothing to prepare us for the realities of later life. The search for meaning outside ourselves must continue, as a personal and individual search for faith about the unknowable. And there is much to be said for undertaking that task of experiencing and learning for ourselves, as well as creating institutions to help us in our work. Counseling is at best a surrogate for self-learning. Doing is better than talking.

Finally, I realize that sooner or later decline appears in most of our activities. We have less energy for work, hobbies, travel, and even learning. And yet in response to the largest of questions, questions of love and responsibility, we become older but not less able.

An Existential Postlude

Discussion about the meaning in life's experiences in the late twentieth century is dominated by our belief that individuals are or can be self-motivated and determinative in what they make of their lives and that this is true at any stage of life. I share this belief but would add that, at least in the Western world, there persist some moral clues or directions about what constitutes not only a meaningful life for the individual but "a good life" and "the good society" (or utopia) to be striven for. Individuals may differ on whether these guides are God-given or are inherent in nature or are human efforts to make sense out of what seems a random and painful struggle to survive.

If individuals differ as to details, two abstract themes still have power. One is that life has, or can have, a direction and a purpose and that a purpose most of us can share is that of making life better. The belief that it is possible to make life better drives much of the energy and creativity of the industrial and postindustrial eras. We may not have reached utopia, but it seems to lie ahead. This is implicit in much of religious teaching, modified in recent years by a belief that the future is on earth, not necessarily in heaven.

A second, equally important theme is that central in whatever we may work toward should be concern for the fates of others—for the fates of our families and neighbors and also of the stranger, the helpless, and the different. Our ways of acting on this concern vary and are often neglectful, but they have resonance and have become incorporated in the legal and constitutional framework for our society.

But collective arrangements for caring do not dismiss personal responsibility. There remain private uncertainties, discomforts, and discontent. But a positive and contented life can be found in cherishing how much individuals need each other.

This fills the gap, if one exists, between faith (or belief) and reason.

So as I look at the meaning of life's experiences, I find that looking back there have been some beliefs that were acted on but wholly unconsciously. And looking forward in these later years I find that such beliefs not only have personal and inter-personal consequences but have consequences for the kind of society we can try to realize despite the material and self-centered preoccupations of each day.

NINE

The Search for Meaning in the Later Years: The Views of a Seventy-Four-Year-Old Gerontological Social Worker

Rose Dobrof

EIDTORS' INTRODUCTION In this last chapter Rose Dobrof discusses the search for meaning as she has witnessed it in her many years of work with the aged and as she now witnesses it in herself. Evident in her discussion is the increasing salience of this search as the Third Age, with its potential for activity and busyness, fades.

With the ending of the Third Age, questions arise of what one's life was about, what point it had, and how it mattered. What will I leave behind? A possible answer, with which Dobrof was able to comfort a woman in her care, is that one's life will matter to those who continue and that one lives on in their memories.

There are other questions as well, having to do with how well one has used the time of one's life. These bring with them assessments of actions taken and not taken, of responsibilities met and unmet. Some are content with the lives they led; others are unforgiving toward themselves and despair at the impossibility of correcting the past.

Dobrof, as did Moody in an earlier chapter, quotes both Erikson and Becker. The two together suggest both the difficulties and the importance of the search for meaning in late life: difficulties because finality is so bewildering a concept; importance because we can come to know ourselves as both product and author of our life course.

Dobrof is the founding director of the Hunter/Brookdale Center on Aging in New York City. We are grateful to her for having written this chapter from her double perspective, that of the professional who has worked with the aged for many years and of the person herself in late life. She makes us aware of how the search for meaning comes about, and she helps us to recognize what it feels like to be engaged in it.

When I was 63 in 1987, I presented a paper at the Second Annual Colloquium of the Brookdale Center on Aging of Hunter College, in which I talked about my own aging (Dobrof, 1987). I told the participants in the colloquium, most of whom were friends and colleagues of many years' standing, that I had found the paper a difficult one to write. To explain the difficulty, I said: "I want to share my vision [of aging] with you with honor and honesty; yet the risk, of course, is a self-indulgent, idiosyncratic presentation, which in the end would be an embarrassment to you and to me. My solution to this problem was to share my task with others."

What I had done in preparing to write was to talk with, and listen to, and then in the paper to quote a number of my friends and colleagues (and my then 70-year-old husband) about their experiences of aging; thereby I hoped to avoid the danger of a self-indulgent, idiosyncratic presentation. Now, as I am twelve years farther into my life journey, the editors of this book have asked that I write about "aging as understood from the perspective of an older person. . . . We are particularly interested in exploring those things which provide meaning and how these meanings are expressed."

I hope that I can fulfill the anticipations of the editors. As is so often true in the social science disciplines, which provide key building blocks for the theoretical foundation of gerontology, and so also in gerontology itself, we seem to value most highly rigorously designed research studies with large samples and sophisticated statistical analyses. The individual story, qualitative analyses, the history of one family: these are grist for the mills of *Modern Maturity* or *New Choices* or *Seniority* but not for the pages of the scholarly journals or books of our field. Yet meaning has both objective and subjective aspects. To discuss meaning, we need to look both at commonly held values and at qualities that derive from the life of the individual.

Yet, as I did in 1987, so also now I worry about how useful to others will be what I have to say about my own experience in the search for meaning in these last years of my life. I am twelve years older now; we know from studies and I know from my own experience and those of friends that a sense of inwardness, along with time spent in introspection and review of the past, increases with age. This reflection on self can be the equivalent of or lead to narcissism, from which nothing interesting or helpful to others could emerge, save, perhaps, for a bad example and one not to be emulated. Alternatively, the introspection can bring a deepened understanding of the later years and their significance in the life course of the individual. It can bring a heightened appreciation of these years and the opportunity they provide to find meaning in them and in the years that have gone before. Perhaps the introspection can even lead to wisdom, which is supposed to be a bounty of a long life, well lived.

Despite this sense of inwardness in old age, it appears to me that the search for meaning is a task that begins early in life, perhaps in adolescence, and continues so long as one is sentient, waxing and waning in intensity, sometimes a matter of preoccupation, sometimes only in the background of one's thoughts, sometimes even outside of conscious awareness. However, the search itself and the definition of meaning and the ways meaning is represented are likely to change over the years. Flora Maxwell talks of the special "intensity" of the search in the later years (Maxwell, 1991). I think of the word "poignancy" to describe how it feels to me: the search is, I believe, deeply affecting but also often disturbing or distressing in ways that I think are not so characteristic of it at earlier stages of life.

I want to return to this matter of the special intensity of the search during the later years of life, but first let me write about the "life review" that Robert N. Butler, M.D., first posited in the early 1960s (Butler, 1963). As the readers of this book probably remember, Butler argued that reminiscence, the "remembrance of things past" of Marcel Proust, was a normal process all during the life cycle. For older persons, it became a vehicle for the "life review," an important aspect of the individual's recognition that life was drawing to a close and an important way of facing and reducing the anxiety most of us experience as we face our own mortality. Butler wrote about reminiscence and the life review as "spontaneous, unselective," and universal, with a "special intensity and emphasis on putting one's life in order."

Besides writing about life review as a normal process, Butler and his colleague and wife Myrna Lewis studied and wrote about it as a therapeutic intervention, as a method professionals could employ to help older people face the last great challenge of life: their own deaths (Lewis & Butler, 1964). In this chapter, my intellectual debt to Butler and Lewis is evident. Like them, I see the life review as a universal process of living that is both normal and lifelong; I think of it also, as the reader will see in my later discussion of Mrs. M., Mrs. S., Mr. G., and Mr. W., as a therapeutic tool in our work with older people. For me, the life review is an essential component in our search for meaning, a way of examining and reexamining our life goals and commitments that is, in the end, necessary to our understanding and acceptance of the lives we have lived.

One more item about Butler's earliest writings about reminiscence and the life review: I joined the staff of the Hebrew Home for the Aged at Riverdale, New York, in April 1961, thus beginning my career in the field of aging. The 407 residents and patients in the home the day I began were mostly in their seventies and eighties, and almost all had been born in the shtetls of Poland and Russia and had come to the United States in the last decades of the nineteenth century or the pre–World War I years of the twentieth century. They had settled on the Lower East Side of Manhattan, and most of the men and some of the women had worked in the then flourishing garment industry in New York City. Almost all had married, most had children and grandchildren, and some had great-grandchildren. Not surprisingly, the majority of our residents and patients were women.

For me, who had been born and raised in Denver, Colorado, and had never come to New York even as a visitor until moving here in 1960, the residents in the home represented a world I knew about only from books. I was eager to learn about that world, and I loved listening to the stories our residents told about their lives. But I was warned by some of the staff, "It's not good for them to remember the past. They get depressed." And when I said that they seemed to want to talk about their life experiences, one staff member told me what I needed to do: "Divert them. Change the subject. Get them to go to an activity like arts and crafts."

I was certain that my colleagues who didn't believe in encouraging our residents to talk about their pasts were wrong; several of us at the home believed that reminiscing was normal and often therapeutic for the older people who lived there. But it was not until we read Dr. Butler's writing about the life review, particularly the 1963 article just cited, that we received validation for our position from an authority whose credentials our colleagues couldn't question. I still remember how Dr. Butler's articles freed us to encourage residents to tell their stories to us. I remember also how excited we were when we saw how the residents' life reviews had helped them put their houses in order through remembering and reflecting on their pasts. So, more than thirty years ago, my own experience convinced me that the life review was both an important activity in our search for meaning and a useful therapeutic intervention.

Now to return to a discussion of the intensity and the poignancy of the search for meaning in old age: these characteristics of the search are, I think, connected to the inescapable recognition in old age that time is short, that, in the words of Erik Erikson (1950), "[one must accept that] one's one and only life cycle [is] something that had to be and that by necessity, permitted of no substitutions" (p. 268). And if one does not achieve Erikson's "accrued ego integration," then "the one and only life cycle is not accepted as the ultimate of life. Despair expresses the feeling that the time is now short, too short for the attempt to start another life and to try out alternate roads to integrity" (p. 269).

Here Erikson is describing despair as the psychic price individuals pay if they are unable to negotiate successfully their eighth age, if they are not able in old age to accept the inevitability of their own life cycle. But decades later Erikson, now an old man, wrote somewhat differently—a difference that I think reflected the fact that he (and his wife, Joan, with whom he wrote) were now themselves in the eighth decade of life. Now Erikson writes about "grand-generativity," a state different from, although related to, "generativity," one of the poles of maturity he had written about in the 1950s. In contrast to the polarity of "ego integrity versus despair" which he had earlier said characterized the last age of life, he now proposes that "[t]he capacity for grand-generativity . . . contributes to the individual's struggle to transcend realistic despair as the end of life approaches, inevitably" (Erikson, Erikson, & Kivnick, 1986, pp. 74–75).

I believe that Erikson was right when he wrote of the despair that blights the lives of those who are not able to accept that what was, was; who live out their last days, weeks, months, years wishing that things had been different, regretting and bewailing both their sins of omission and their sins of commission. Mark Twain was mistaken when he wrote that in old age we're more likely to regret what we didn't do than what we did; people regret both.

I think the difference between what Erikson wrote in the 1950s and what he wrote in 1986 is not trivial. I believe that he is later saying something equally correct but different from his earlier proposal of a last polarity of ego-integrity and despair when he writes about the "realistic despair" that accompanies the recognition that time is short.

My sense is that in his earlier context, Erikson thought despair to be avoidable, if only we can accept the historic inevitability of our one life cycle. We may, in our old age, feel such despair because we have not been able to put our houses in order: to understand and forgive ourselves for the wrongs we committed, the errors we made. Despair may indeed for some of us be the horrific price we pay for those mistakes and harmful things we have done. And if we are not able to accept our "one and only life cycle . . . as the ultimate of life," then we are doomed to live always in fear of death.

I wonder about the possibility of avoidance of some measure of despair. Even allowing for the infinite variety among human beings in their life experiences, in how they define meaning, in how avidly they search for it, in how important the search is to them—even allowing for all of this, I doubt that there are many human beings who are not at some times and to some degree bedeviled by thoughts of what might have been, of roads not taken, and responsibilities not fulfilled.

But this is quite different, I think, from the recognition of despair as a realistic and well-nigh universal and altogether human response, not to regret or guilt but rather to the knowledge that there is not much time left on earth for us. What I am saying is that for many of us, there is the wish for more time to walk this earth, to live our lives, to participate, in the words of Oliver Wendell Holmes, in "the action and passion of [our] time."

So a certain amount of despair, I think, goes with the territory of old age; it is not simply the price we pay for sins and errors of the past. The question becomes: How do we prevent despair from becoming the blight of the later years? How do we make these years, in Carl Jung's words, more "than a pitiful appendage to life's morning."

From my experiences in the home, here is an example of the search for meaning, for resolution, as time grows short. I sat for a time beside the bed of Mrs. M., a resident whom I had come to love and to respect in the years I had known her. She was dying; we both knew it; and her question was "Is this all there is? Is there nothing more?" She was a secularist: religion, the hope of an afterlife, a belief in God and in his purpose—these comforts were denied her. And so her question: "Is this all?"

Over the last weeks of her life, until she sank into her final coma, she sought the answers to her question, and for that which gave meaning to her life. She recalled people and events: her journey to New York City from the shtetl in Poland where she was born, the tenement she lived in, the factory where she worked until she married, her husband, the children, her sisters and brother. She remembered the day when she became a citizen, and she remembered elections and strikes and picnics and movies that she had loved and stars whom she admired. (Did I, for example, remember Paul Muni, and did I know that he was Jewish?) And she remembered the day her husband died in the 1930s and how she had to go to work so that the children could stay in school. She recalled vividly their high school graduations, and she talked with special pride about the two who went on to college.

I reminded her at one point that now her three children are married and have grown children of their own and that two of her children are themselves grandparents. She said, "And they're good people, aren't they, Rose? You know them." I agreed. I did know them. They were good people, devoted to their mother. "Maybe this is all there is," Mrs. M. said in one of our conversations. "There's the family, work, good times, troubles, all that happens. Maybe this is it."

Maybe she was right, I said, and then I talked about how proud she could feel about what she had accomplished in her life, about what a good person she was, about how sweet would be the memories of her that her children and grandchildren would have—and that I would have, also. "It's not so much," she said at one point during our talks, "but maybe it's enough."

I think back often to the older people I knew during my nine years on the staff of the home and of how much I learned about life from them. I think of the conversations I have just recounted. I know that Mrs. M. felt despair as she faced the end of her life, that there were times when she didn't feel that "family, work, good times . . . " were enough to give her life the meaning she sought. But I also know that despair was not all she felt; that in the end, she knew why she had lived. The meaning of her life was represented in her children and their children, and her legacy was to be their memories of her.

In the Book of Job, Bildad describes the fate of the wicked:

> His remembrance shall perish from the earth,
> And he shall have no name abroad.
> He shall be driven from light into darkness,
> And chased out of the world.

Mrs. M. did not die in despair, for she knew that her remembrance would not perish, and it was in this knowledge that I think she found the essential meaning of her life. And for many older people, I believe that their certain knowledge that they will live on in the memories of their children and others whose lives they touched gives their lives meaning and purpose and significance. This may be particularly true for those like Mrs. M.—and me—who cannot find a divine purpose for our lives.

A less happy memory for some of my colleagues and me is the memory of Mr. G., who sat every day in a chair in the hall in front of the nurses' station in the infirmary unit where he was a patient. He never spoke, never smiled, never responded, even by gesture, to the efforts of staff to connect with him. I don't remember how we learned his story: probably from the rabbi who was responsible for his coming to the Home to live. Mr. G, like Mrs. M., was from Poland, but he did not come to the United States until the 1930s. He left his wife and children behind, promising to send for them as soon as he earned the money for their transportation. That time never came, and all of his family perished in the Holocaust.

My memory is that he did not learn of their fate until after World War II, that until then he clung to the hope that somehow they would be among the survivors. Once hope was gone, Mr. G. lived with an unbearable burden of guilt, a burden of which he could not, would not speak, even to our Polish-born medical director or the rabbi or to any of the nurses and social workers who wanted so desperately to help Mr. G. escape the despair with which he lived each day.

Day after day, Mr. G. sat, his silence and his sad eyes haunting all of us, and our inability to help him was a burden and a sorrow to all of us. On our staff were two people who finally were able to break Mr. G.'s silence, although never were they able to crack the wall of his despair. They were an aide who, like Mr. G., had escaped Hitler's Europe and a researcher who read Dr. Butler's work and believed that if Mr. G. could remember the historical context of his decision to leave his family, if he could think of the fact that they were among millions who perished, and if he could remember also how hard he worked to save enough money to bring his wife and children here, he might be able to forgive himself.

And so, day after day, the two staff talked with Mr. G., read articles to him that they hoped would help him understand that he had done the best he could, took him to visit with the medical director and the rabbi, brought him a new shirt and tie at Chanukah time, and took him for walks outside in good weather. Mr. G. never did escape the bleakness of his despair and never could bring himself to accept the historical inevitability of his one life, but he did end his years of silence in conversations with the two staff who loved him. And when he died, still despairing, at least there were the two women and the rabbi at his bedside, giving him the forgiveness and the absolution that he could not give himself.

And then there was Mr. W., the widowed father of three children in their fifties. The children brought Mr. W. to the home for his initial interview. When the social worker saw them separate from their father, they were painfully frank in their description of his life and their relationships with him. They described him as "distant," "selfish," "never there for us or our mother," and "thinking only of himself and his comfort." After their mother's death some years before, they had maintained only minimal and infrequent contact with him. "We did what we had to—no more."

They assured us that they would continue to do what had to be done, but they wanted us to understand that what they would do, they would do as a duty, not out of love or respect for the father who had never loved them. And so Mr. W. entered the home, and, alas, we found ourselves feeling sympathy for his children. He wasn't a lovable man: he was always first in line, making certain that he was taken care of, given to, attended well.

One of my most vivid memories of Mr. W. was during the great blackout of 1965. The men on the staff were helping the most frail among our residents to get down the stairs to the first floor of the building, which was lighted by an auxiliary generator. Mr. W. was not frail or ill; nonetheless he had secured the assistance of two of the staff, while Mr. S., who had a serious heart condition, was negotiating the stairs on his own, clinging to the banister and stopping every few steps to rest and catch his breath.

This was Mr. W., and it was often difficult for staff to treat him with the respect and understanding that were due all residents. In our staff conferences, our psychiatrist talked of Mr. W.'s troubled and deprived childhood and tried to help the staff understand that what we saw as selfishness and coldness was the mask Mr. W. wore to protect himself against the emptiness of his life and the despair which he fought to keep from his conscious thoughts.

This was one time when the staff who argued in favor of diverting residents from remembering may have been right. A young member of the social work staff learned from Mr. W. that he had played the violin in his youth. At the social worker's behest, a violin was procured for Mr. W. It would be nice to write that Mr. W. had real talent and that his violin playing worked miracles in his relationships with his children and with other residents. The truth is that he was a terrible violinist. But, oh, how he worked at his playing, and how content he seemed when he was playing. The day came when Mr. W. announced that he was ready to play before an audience, and we were all dragooned by our colleague into attending his recital. She was even able to persuade his children to attend.

The music was scratchy and riddled with mistakes and false

starts, but that hour on a Sunday afternoon in the dining room of the home before an audience of his family and some staff and residents was probably one of the high points of Mr. W.'s sad life. I can still remember the glow on his face, the bows he took, the tribute he paid to his social worker. He continued his daily playing until he suffered a fatal heart attack some months after the concert. In the drawer in his bedside table, we found a handwritten note in which he asked that his violin—"my most precious possession"—be given to his "best friend," his social worker.

As I think now of Mr. W., gone these three decades, my guess is that he never thought back on his life, that, indeed, he used his psychic energy to block out memories of the past, to escape feelings of emptiness and alienation and despair. His violin playing was all-engrossing; my memory of his concert includes my sense that he was unaware of the mixed response of his audience. The violin gave him surcease from internal pain, as nothing else could.

I wonder now if, had we been more skilled therapists, had more sophisticated psychotropic drugs been available, could we somehow have breached the walls that separated him from his family and from all of us except his best friend, the social worker? Could we have helped him accept his one life, find meaning in it, put his house in order?

I don't know. I only know that Mr. W.'s violin playing helped him keep the demons of despair and regret and guilt and sorrow at bay and that the playing filled the time of his last years and gave some meaning to those years. And I know also that Mr. W. was right in the end: the social worker was his best friend, and it was right that he left his prize possession to her.

I knew during my time at the home, and particularly with people like Mrs. M., that residents and staff were often together searching for answers to questions about purpose and meaning. Over the years since then, my thoughts return to the home and to people from whom I learned about life and about death. I thought I understood then what our search was about, but now that I am as old as many of the residents were, and now that I am the mother of grown children and a grandmother, and now that my husband and I and our friends are facing the reality that time is short and that we cannot create alternative paths, there are new dimensions to my understanding and a special poignancy to my own search for answers.

I think in this context of the words of T. S. Eliot's "Little Gidding":

> We shall not cease
> From exploration
> And the end of all our exploring
> Will be to arrive where we started
> And know the place for the first time.

This is what I think: that consciously and unconsciously, we seek meaning all during our lifetime but that our understanding of the search, even of what it is we seek, changes as we grow older. I thought I understood what Mrs. M. and I were talking about, and I did. But then I was 36, and the urgency that I feel now, I did not feel then. Or, rather, I felt that urgency for Mrs. M., not for me.

And now I have arrived where I started, but it is different. Now I think I understand in ways that I didn't when I was younger. I know the place for the first time. I also acknowledge with humility how much about life I don't understand. And I suspect that my understanding of tomorrow may be different from my apprehension of today: mediated by my memories of the past but from a new perspective, and perhaps, as now, with painful recognition of how little I understand.

I think that Erikson was correct in his emphasis on the despair we may feel if, unlike Mrs. M., we cannot claim the legacy we are leaving behind, and I think he was also right in his later discussion of the inevitable despair that comes as we face the inevitability of our death. Ernest Becker (1973) captured what I am talking about best, I think. As Moody has noted, in an earlier chapter in this book, Becker made vivid the existential paradox that in our lives we have a splendid uniqueness but with death we disappear forever.

It is, I believe, this existential paradox that is the source of our despair, and also the matrix for our search. And if our later years are more than just an appendage to the years that went before, if they are meaningful in their own right, it is because they provide us with the time and need for reflection, for remembering, for thinking about what our lives were all about, even for achieving the wisdom that can come from experience.

REFERENCES

Becker, E. (1973). *The denial of death.* New York: Free Press.
Butler, R. N. (1963). The life review: An interpretation of reminiscence in the aged. *Psychiatry, 26,* 65–76.
Dobrof, R. (1987). The aging of a gerontologist. *Pride Institute Journal of Long Term Home Health Care, 6*(3).
Erikson, E. H. (1950). Eight ages of man. In *Childhood and society* (pp. 168–169). New York: Norton.
Erikson, E. H., Erikson, J. M., & Kivnick, H. Q. (1986). *Vital involvement in old age.* New York: Norton.
Lewis, M., & Butler, R. N. (1964). Life review therapy: Putting memories to work in individual and group therapy. *Geriatrics, 29,* 165–169.
Maxwell, F. (1991). The measure of my days. In M. Fowler & P. McCutcheon (Eds.), *Songs of experience* (pp. 22–26). New York: Ballantine Books.

Epilogue: Concluding Note on Meaning and the Possibility of Productive Aging

Robert S. Weiss and Scott A. Bass

Issues of meaning are important throughout life but may well be problematic only for the young and the old. Adolescents, not yet decided on their lifework or whether, let alone who, they will marry, can obsess both alone and in bull sessions with peers about the direction their lives will take. Once adult responsibilities are assumed, people seem to go on automatic pilot, except for those intervals of midlife crisis when the point of it all may be reconsidered. In later life, with occupational and familial tasks completed, grand questions of the meaning of life again have personal relevance. There is again opportunity, if not need, to ask, "What is it all about?"

One of the discoveries made by many in later life is how much it matters to them that they matter to others. They find, sometimes to their surprise, that the marginality that accompanies retirement makes them uncertain of their worth. Their past success provides inadequate support for their current self-esteem. Their earlier feelings of worth proved unbankable. The comment is sometimes made by retired people who had achieved some prominence in their occupations: "I've gone from who's who to who's he?"

Others, however, appear indifferent to no longer counting in the world of their work. They find meaning in the routines of family life and in the gratifying and broadening experiences of voluntary activity, travel, and participation in programs of instruction. Their lives seem adequately meaningful despite only limited responsibilities.

What does it mean to experience one's life as meaningful? It means something different from having goals. The goal of fixing up a summer place so it can serve as a year-round residence can occupy thought and energy yet not be enough to make one feel that one's life still matters. And a life of retreat, perhaps associated with a religious order, can be meaningful even without evident personal goals. Having meaning in life has to do with feeling that one still matters, to oneself at least, and that what one does makes sense. It has to do with the conviction that one's life is about something more than simply surviving.

Sociologists sometimes divide up the activities engaged in by organizations into those that are required to keep the organization going and those that advance the organization's program. The same categorization can be made of people's activities. Much of later life is given to maintenance activities, to staying healthy and alert. But for most people it would seem that for life to be meaningful there has to be something more: an emotional investment, a commitment.

From our earliest days as functioning humans we want to engage with the world around us. As Marris points out in his chapter, we begin with a readiness, and a need, to maintain the close relationships that bring with them feelings of security. But once those relationships are in place, we want to explore and to encounter and master challenge. We want to make a difference in the world around us. That drive to engage with the world and to make a difference in it is at the core of children's play and adults' work. The drive to engage persists, for most of us, into the Third Age and beyond.

Our society provides few hints regarding how engagement might be managed in the Third Age. We may no longer picture those retired from work as miserly or dotty, or as curmudgeons or dependents. But the new images of the aged—the carefree tourist, the golfer, the benign but essentially unburdened grandparent—are equally without social concern. Rubinstein, in his chapter, points out that the concept of a "Third Age" is, among other things, an effort to redefine the postretirement phase of life as one of opportunity for self-expression rather than bitter or addled self-protection. But the new social expectation is like the expectation that preceded it in that it assumes a later life without vital involvement in the social world. Indeed, elders may be told that their separation from the labor force has been earned through their years of work, as though social irrelevance is an appropriate reward for a career's contributions.

American institutions and businesses that are designed specifically for the elderly encourage the perception that the elderly have entered into an endless vacation. Guttman's discussion of the functioning of older men in Druse society suggests what might be an alternative. Although a society that honors older men but not older women is an imperfect model, Druse society provides at least its older men with valued, respected roles. These roles honor the experience and maturity that comes with age. Here is a social institution that meets genuine needs of its society by using the abilities distinct to the able aged, which include not only wisdom based on experience but also time freed from the demands of parenthood and labor.

Insofar as we in this country see elders engaged with our social institutions, it is as consumers. Our institutions include programs such as Elderhostel that provide cultural, educational, and travel opportunities for the active elderly; senior centers with sometimes extensive menus of social and cultural activities; college programs in which seniors can pursue learning without sitting for examinations; and such activities for the elderly as golf clubs, bridge clubs, crafts programs, and classes in which seniors are coached in writing or in the arts. In any of these programs the older person may well find self-enrichment but little opportunity for contributing to others in ways that matter.

This is not to say that we in this country have no models at all for what might be a vital, productive later life. However, our models are of exceptional people. We have biographies of eminent men and women who maintained their effectiveness to an advanced age: Oliver Wendell Holmes and Susan B. Anthony are two among many. And we have popular books that describe men and women in later life who would still be seen as unusual if their ages were halved: they direct large enterprises or undertake adventuresome travel or are successful writers and poets or participate actively in sport. People who are more nearly ordinary may find inspiration in such accounts but are unlikely to find guidance. They will lack the prerequisites of already established social position, wealth, talent, or skill that these exceptional people have.

Can Americans, despite limited, or absent, institutional support, find meaning in later life? Many find satisfaction in daily activities—which is not the same as meaning—but they also, often, find a way of contributing to others in their social worlds, of continuing to make a difference. Cohler and Hostetler, in their chapter, describe the lives of two men without children, one living in a distinctly nontraditional but highly stable intimate partnership, the other living more or less alone, though again in a nontraditional lifestyle, each content with life, vital, and engaged. Each continues to contribute energy to the functioning of his community and to accept responsibility for people to whom he is close. Each appears to find meaning in this way of life.

The existentialist writer Albert Camus suggested that people could count their lives meaningful to the extent that they had been engaged in the struggles of their time and place. It is, of course, too grand an expectation for most of us that we measure ourselves by our contribution to the larger struggles of our time: the amelioration of poverty, the settling of peoples, the reduction of ethnic strife, the taming of the scourges of illness and disability, the extension of understanding. Enough, for most of us, that we have participated fully and honestly in the smaller struggles of life: that we have done constructive work, have raised a family, and have been faithful to those who depended on us. Enough, for most of us, that we have tried, and continue to try, to fashion a better society in the milieu within which we live.

Moody, in his chapter in this book, notes that both Erikson and Jung proposed that the meaningfulness of a life is to be found in its continuing fidelity to core values. In Erikson's formulation, the well-being of the aged required first that they have met the test of generativity, which might be phrased as contributing to the repair and progress of their society. It would then require that they have met the test of integrity. Integrity is a more difficult concept. It suggests being all of a piece, youth and maturity, values and actions. It also suggests the ability to review one's one and only life and conclude that it had point and coherence and was good enough.

Any number of factors play a role in deciding whether a particular person can achieve any of this. In this book Settersten reviews the extensive research that has been done on what produces the particular meanings given to later life and what makes it easier or more difficult to express those meanings. He shows that factors include, most broadly, the messages carried by people's society and culture about what is to be expected of them at various points in their lives and also the social positions that provide some opportunities and close off others. Familial and occupational relationships encourage only certain ways of understanding what life is about. They are needed sources of support, but they can also be sources of constraint. Still, as Rowles and Ravdal show, people do best where there is continuity of physical and social contexts, and even constraints can help sustain direction.

What advice might be offered to those entering the Third Age? How should they ensure that their lives continue to be meaningful? We might begin by noting that we must concern ourselves both with goals and with process. Goals are the point of it all, the achievement to which energy is devoted. The activities of later life can be meaningful only as they contribute to valued ends: making life better for grandchildren, helping a church to function, relieving the distress of the ill, or raising money for a cause. But meaningfulness also resides in the processes through which goals are sought. A meaningful activity would be one that captures a person's energies so that the person is entirely engaged by it. It would provide Csikszentmihalyi's "flow," in which the actor is so immersed in the activity that self-awareness is lost.

That goals and process are necessary to each other is made evident in the autobiographical reports of Morris and Dobrof. Each pursued careers aimed at bettering the world, and each found that their efforts were absorbing and gratifying. Our advice to the person entering the Third Age would be, then, not only to get involved but to get involved with an enterprise that matters to you.

Where might one find an enterprise that matters? A first thought is to return attention to the world of work, the world that was left on entrance into the Third Age. It is here that meaningful activity is likely to have been found earlier in life; it is most likely to be here that meaningful activity can continue to be found.

The older person may well have something unique to offer. Rather like the older Druse man, the older person can provide continuity to an enterprise. To be sure, in many fields technical obsolescence is an inescapable accompaniment of seniority. Yet those who have had long experience in a field are likely to have a repertoire of still applicable problem-solving approaches that constitutes a kind of usable wisdom. Further, older people, more than the young, are attracted by flexible hours and part-time work and can provide employers with a kind of reserve labor force available to be tapped as needed.

A growing body of literature discusses the benefits of "productive aging," by which is meant aging in which the elderly remain engaged in activities of social worth, whether these are paid or not (e.g., Bass, Caro, & Chen, 1993). Productive aging can be seen as an approach to a meaningful later life that emphasizes continued constructive functioning in the society. Yet, as Matilda White Riley has observed, the social institutions of our society often lag behind changes in the life experience or the values of its members (e.g., Riley, Kahn, & Foner, 1994). We are in need of institutions that would provide opportunities for some of our elderly to continue to play valid and valued roles in our society.

Many people in their sixties and seventies who no longer need to work, and may indeed have been encouraged by both their firms and their families not to work, and who are no longer responsible for raising children, are in other ways little changed from the responsible figures they had been a decade or two earlier. Many of them would value opportunities to continue to use their skills and energies productively.

There are, of course, others in the Third Age for whom social irrelevance is fine. They may always have made family the center of their lives, and spending time with family is now enough for them. Or earlier in their lives they found both gratification and meaning in the competition and camaraderie of golf or bridge, and continue to do so. But for many in the Third Age, continuity requires being needed and valued by others for social contribution. Without opportunity for social contribution, they can feel themselves to be wasting their skills and energies and betraying their very selves. As some of them put it, they are not ready for the shelf.

A kind of logic can be discerned in our society's absence of interest in the possible contributions of the elderly. The amazing gains in productivity brought about by an educated, motivated workforce, augmented by automation, robotics, and the other developments of computers, have led to a situation in which there may seem to be no need for the contributions that could be made by the elderly. If our society really must deal with a surplus of workers, it can seem to make sense for those of retirement years to only tend to their families, their hobbies, their trips, and themselves and leave to younger people the work that must be done.

Yet our society can ill afford to send into comfortable exile its veteran managers and professionals and craftsmen. By doing so our society loses the people who carry in their minds the histories of their fields, the concerns of earlier practitioners, and the developments of practice, goals, and ethics they have witnessed in their careers. It loses the people who can bring perspective to those preoccupied with the problems of the moment and who can tell them, in response to many particular problems, what has been tried and what has failed.

Certainly, many of those in the Third Age would themselves be best served by continuing to contribute to the enterprises that mattered to them during their work lives. It would undoubtedly make sense to them that their contribution should be different from what it had been earlier, that they should function as consultants rather than operatives, that they should be on call or available only part-time rather than obligated to a daily commute. But if their contribution were truly valuable, they would have a valid basis for the respect of others, for self-respect, and for a sense that they continued to matter. They would be elders in a community that for most continues to matter deeply, the community of their lifelong work.

As has been noted, not everyone in the Third Age will want to remain engaged with the world of their former work or to commit themselves to "productive aging." On the contrary, they may find most gratifying a later life in which they are relieved of the responsibilities they once carried. We must respect the different ways people will want to use their years in the Third Age and, in particular, recognize and respect those for whom an attraction of the Third Age is its potential for freedom from all obligation.

However, our society needs greater recognition than now exists of the experience, knowledge, and skills that those entering the Third Age are taking with them. For the sake of all of us, our industry and our other institutions should provide opportunities for useful and responsible positions to those in the Third Age for whom meaningfulness requires that they continue to make a difference.

REFERENCES

Bass, S. A., Caro, F. G., & Chen, Y.-P. (Eds.). (1993). *Achieving a productive aging society.* Westport, CT: Auburn House.
Riley, M. W., Kahn, R. L., & Foner, A. (1994). *Age and structural lag: Society's failure to provide meaningful opportunities in work, family, and leisure.* New York: Wiley.

Index

military service, 142–143,
    166–167
Mings, Robert C., 98
Moore, Thomas, 47
music, 184–185

narcissism, 38, 44, 175
neighborhoods, 86, 88, 95
Neugarten, Bernice, 46, 63
New Age, 46, 47
New Passages (Sheehy), 45–46
Norris-Baker, Carolyn, 94
nursing homes, 70, 84, 90,
    91, 96

O'Bryant, Shirley L., 85
Ochberg, Richard, 139
old age
  and continuing need for
    adaptation, 14, 15 (*see also*
    relocation)
  and declining health, 59, 63,
    67–68, 69, 96, 97–98,
    145–146, 162
  differences in, between
    societies, 58–60, 115–117,
    131–135
  and historical knowledge,
    25–26
  See also aging; Third Age
Older Americans Act, 90
Omega Institute, 46
oral history, 26

Parkes, Colin Murray, 16
Parmelee, Patricia A., 96–97

part-time employment, 8, 64,
    195
Passages (Sheehy), 43, 44, 152
Passive Mastery, 126, 128, 132, 133
Patten, Simon, 164
Peale, Norman Vincent, 47
Perkins, Douglas D., 104
photographs, 81, 93, 103
placelessness, 89, 106
"place-making," 84
"place therapy," 103
popular culture, 29, 149, 152–153
  and images of aging, 29, 37
  See also aging: popular
    writings on
possessions, 81–82, 87–88,
    101–102
post–World War II era, 41,
    90–91, 95, 142
poverty, 22–23, 32
Power of Positive Thinking, The
    (Peale), 47
preliterate societies, 117–118,
    129–130
"productive aging," 195, 197
Project A. G. E. (Age,
    Generation, and
    Experience), 58–60
Proust, Marcel, 176
public policy, 63, 90–91
Pynoos, Jon, 91

Reagan, Ronald, 44–45, 47
Redfield, James, 47
reengagement, 132–133
regret, 179

territoriality, 90

Thematic Apperception Test
    (TAT), 125–126, 127, 129, 131

therapeutic intervention,
    176–178, 180–186

Third Age, 3–12, 29–39
    and cohort identity, 33–34
    contexts for meaning in, 35–36
    defined, 3, 29, 31, 36, 39
    developmental ambiguity of,
        33–34
    farther edge of, 39, 161, 173, 191
    and "life review," 11, 35–36, 56
    limited societal recognition of,
        10–11, 29
    multiple options available in,
        3, 4–5, 9–10, 29–30, 34–35,
        197
    as new historical phenome-
        non, 4, 29, 30, 37
    prerequisites for, 3–4, 29,
        32–33
    and service to others, 9–10,
        161, 169–170

"time budgets of adulthood," 62

Titanic, 46

Townsend, Peter, 22–23

traditional societies, 11, 117–118,
    132–133. *See also* Druse
    society

travel, 9, 164

"tripartition of the life course,"
    60

Twain, Mark, 179

volunteer work, 65–66, 146, 150,
    164

voting, 65

wealth, national, 4

Weil, Andrew, 47

Wheeler, W. Michael, 99

Why Survive? (Butler), 42

widowhood, 18, 19, 20, 21, 34, 69

Williamson, Marianne, 47

wisdom, 26, 27, 46, 175

women, 22, 63, 64, 69. *See also*
    sex differences

Wong, Paul, 61

work. *See* employment;
    volunteer work

World War II, 62, 166, 182

young-old. *See* Third Age